THE GOOD, THE BAD, THE COOKBOOK

Just Cook It!

THE GOOD, THE BAD, THE COOKBOOK

A SINFUL GUIDE TO HEALTHY COOKING

MARIO J. PORRECA
KIRK KOLICH

FOREWORD BY

DR. JOSEPH D. PORRECA

LANGDON STREET PRESS MINNEAPOLIS

Copyright © 2011 by Mario J. Porreca and Kirk Kolich

Langdon Street Press
212 3rd Avenue North, Suite 290
Minneapolis, MN 55401
612.455.2293
www.langdonstreetpress.com

All rights reserved. No part of this publication may be reproduced, stored in a retrieval system, or transmitted, in any form or by any means, electronic, mechanical, photocopying, recording, or otherwise, without the prior written permission of the author.

ISBN-13: *978-1-936782-62-8*
LCCN: *2011937781*

Distributed by Itasca Books

Book design by Kristeen Wegner

All images, unless otherwise noted, are property of the author. ©Mario's Menu, LLC

Printed in the United States of America

To Dr. Joe and Denise Porreca and Gus and Jacqueline Kolich.

Thank you for your constant love and support in all that we do and in all that we strive to accomplish. Without you, we would not be where we are today, figuratively and literally.

In Loving Memory of John and Agnes Kolich, Elmer Dranusky, Joseph Jupina, and Josephine Porreca. You are always missed and never forgotten.

CONTENTS

Foreword by Dr. Joseph D. Porreca, DC xi
Introduction xii
A Note on Using This Book xiii
Mario's Menu Basic Facts xvi

SECTION I: HORS D'OEUVRES

Grape Balls with Gorgonzola Cheese 3
Cajun Pork Tenderloin with Blue Cheese Honey Dipping Sauce 5
Stuffed Crimini Mushrooms 7
Crab and Avocado Salad 9
Portobello Mushroom Bruschetta 11
King Crab and Brie Bruschetta 13
Shrimp Scampi Dip 15
Peanut Chicken Salad 17
Turkey Saltimbocca with Basil Pesto Dipping Sauce 19

SECTION II: BREAKFAST

Whole-Grain Breakfast Porridge 23
Stuffed French Toast with Blueberry Honey 25
Breakfast Casserole 29
Steak and Eggs with Asiago Cream Sauce 31
Chicken and Sun-Dried Tomato Omelet 33

SECTION III: SOUPS

Chilled Strawberry, Banana, and Vanilla Bean Soup 37
Red Bell Pepper Soup 39
Pear and Parsnip Bisque 41
Sweet 5-Onion Soup with Gruyere Cheese Croustade 43
Wild Mushroom and White Bean Soup 45
Chilled Seafood Gazpacho 47

SECTION IV: SALADS

Strawberry Fennel Salad with White Balsamic Vinaigrette 50
Grilled Romaine Salad with Whole-Wheat Croustade and Creamy
    Avocado-Lemon Dressing 54
Roasted Chicken and Apple Salad with Pomegranate–Poppy Seed Vinaigrette 58
Pittsburgh Steak Salad with Scallion Buttermilk Ranch Dressing 62
Roasted Turkey Cobb Salad with Cranberry-Orange Dressing 66
Blackened Salmon Salad with Lemon-Dill Dressing 70
Mango-Jicama Slaw with Pickled Ginger Vinaigrette 75
Oven-Roasted Summer Potato Salad 77
Creamy Caprese Salad with Basil Ranch Dressing 79

SECTION V: SANDWICHES

Turkey-Apricot Sliders with Fresh Pickles 82
Crab Cake Sliders with Orange-Mustard Aioli 86
Cajun Beef Sliders with Creamy Chimichurri 90
Grilled Vegetable Sandwich with Roasted Shallot Hummus 94
Shrimp and Egg Salad Sandwich 98

SECTION VI: ENTRÉES

Chili-Glazed Turkey Steaks 105
    Sweet Potato Lyonnaise 106
    Grilled Asparagus 107
Horseradish-Crusted Salmon 108
    Papaya-Ginger Sauce 109
    Red Beet Couscous 110
    Roasted Cauliflower and Sugar Snap Peas 111
Rolled Vegetable Lasagna with Basil-Pesto Cream 114
Crabmeat-Stuffed Flounder 119
    Stewed Tomatoes and Fennel 121
    Basil Smashed Red Skin Potatoes 122
    Medley of Yellow Squash and Green Beans 123
Cashew and Coconut–Crusted Chicken Breast 124
    Peach and Chili Sauce 125
    Stir-Fry Vegetables 126
Bacon-Wrapped Mesquite-Marinated Pork Loin 130
    Dried Cranberry Sauce 131
    Sweet Corn and Red Pepper Risotto 132
    Pan-Roasted Butternut Squash and Brussels Sprouts 133
Porcini-Dusted Filet Mignon of Beef 136
    Steak Sauce 137
    Cauliflower Puree 138
    Wilted Arugula with Sun-dried Tomatoes 139
Whole-Wheat Gnocchi with Portobello Mushroom Cream and Tarragon Croissant 142
Creole Chicken Chili with Whole-Grain Cheddar Croutons 149
Vegetable Roulade with Sun-Dried Tomato Cream 153

SECTION VII: THE BAD

Deep-Fried Turkey Saltimbocca with Basil Pesto Dipping Sauce 161

Peanut Butter and Jelly Grape Balls 162

Roasted Shallot and Blue Cheese Dip 163

Spicy Langoustine Cheese Ball 165

Spicy Sausage and 5-Cheese Dip 167

Artichoke and Spinach Dip 169

Goldfish-Crusted Cheesy Potatoes 171

Bacon Mushroom Cheeseburger Casserole 172

Italian Pinwheels 176

Asian-Style Chicken Wings 181

About the Authors 182

FOREWORD

I was extremely honored when the authors of this book asked me to write the foreword. I'm also extremely proud of and impressed with the total body of work. Being a health-care professional for over 25 years, I have come to realize how supremely important a proper diet is to one's health. It has been said that food is the most powerful drug that we put into our bodies, and most of us are putting food into our bodies at least three times daily. You may be thinking to yourself, *Food? A drug?* Exactly! Food acts on your physiology and can affect our health, just as drugs do. If the wrong foods are eaten too often, we eventually suffer the consequences of ill health. What are these consequences? The consequences are that we will be at higher risk for all of the chronic degenerative diseases, such as type-II diabetes, arthritis, heart disease, and even the dreaded *C* word, cancer.

All of the aforementioned diseases are on a steep rise, and the number one thing that we can do to combat this problem is to eat properly and pay more attention to what we ingest on a daily basis. Proper diet is the cornerstone of good health, but who wants to diet? After all, the first three letters in the word diet are *D-I-E*, and most of us, including myself, would rather die than diet. We know that diets do not work; 98 percent of all diets fail. So are we doomed? No, not at all. What does work is applying a little common sense to some healthy lifestyle changes. It doesn't have to be difficult or unpleasant. In fact, eating healthy can be very pleasant. It is not only fun but—as you'll soon discover by utilizing the ideas, suggestions, and recipes in this book—it's delicious too.

It's often been said that the key to life is moderation. I happen to be a firm believer in this philosophy and am pleased to say that this book follows this theme, also. As evidence of this real-world approach to sensible, good eating, you will find many delicious and healthy recipes within these pages. You will also find a few recipes to utilize on those days that you decide to practice moderation and change things up a bit. These recipes were designed mainly to delight your taste buds and allow you to relax and enjoy the gift of wonderful food. Don't get me wrong; the wonderful culinary creations in this book are *all* very delicious. Trust me, I've eaten them all. However, there may be times when you just want to relax and throw caution to the wind. You should definitely have a few "relax days" or "relax meals" built into your life—again, in moderation.

I'm very excited for you to turn the page and begin this wonderful and tasty culinary journey to improved eating and better health. I'm very impressed by the work that has been compiled by these authors. I know they want you to enjoy, relax, and utilize both "the good" and "the bad" in the cookbook. Remember, it's about progress, not perfection.

Yours for Better Health,

Dr. Joseph D. Porreca, DC

INTRODUCTION

As I began writing this introduction to the first Mario's Menu cookbook, I looked to the left of my computer and saw a pretty intimidating sight for most people: two culinary arts books, which I had been using as reference materials while working on this cookbook. These two books alone totaled over 3,000 pages of text, pictures, and different diagrams. I began thinking about the size and quality of the myriad cookbooks and culinary arts books out there. I own a very extensive culinary library and, yes, I have read all of the books that I own. But I am a culinary professional, so that's expected of me. I started to wonder what the average person's library looks like when it comes to food.

So I did what any chef playing detective would do: I started looking. When I was at a friend or family member's home I would look at their cookbooks. The first thing that immediately grabbed my attention was the amount of dust on them! I'm neither a scientist nor a detective, but I would venture to say that the average person owns at least 10 cookbooks and probably only uses one or maybe two recipes from each book. In fact, they have probably prepared these recipes so many times that they no longer have to even consult the books, hence the dust. I am not saying this is true of everyone, but we all have the aunt who brings the same dish to every family function, no matter what. Don't get me wrong, that dish is always delicious and a family favorite by this point, and it should be, considering all the practice preparing it! So I started thinking, *What if we had a cookbook that we could not only use on a consistent basis, but one we also enjoyed using and that contained food that was actually good for you?* It was an epiphany for me, and so my quest began!

I had been working with my former colleague and one of my best friends, Kirk Kolich, an executive chef for Parkhurst Dining Services, doing live healthy-cooking demonstrations to educate people on the importance of healthy eating while still being able to eat great food. So I immediately threw the idea out there for a cookbook. Kirk, who isn't the type of person to get overly excited easily, began throwing ideas at me faster than I could absorb them. We immediately got to work, and it seemed like I lived at his house for two straight months. Almost every day, as soon as he would finish work, we would begin brainstorming ideas and testing recipes in his kitchen. This worked out perfectly, because our goal for this book was that *anyone* could use it to go to the local supermarket and within a half hour buy everything they would need to go home and prepare a great-tasting, healthy meal in a very short amount of time with minimal kitchen skills required. We wanted to create an ordinary person's cookbook that would allow them to produce extraordinary results in the kitchen. So it only made sense to create these recipes in an average home kitchen and even take the pictures of the dishes on an average dining room table.

Kirk and I are very excited about the dishes we created and are even more excited for all of you to begin utilizing these recipes. We set out to create a book that people will actually use, and we believe we have done that. No matter what we believe, this cannot happen unless you actually prepare the recipes. So even more important than the time we spent creating this book is the time you will spend utilizing it. So, please, get in the kitchen and get busy—wow your family and friends, and enjoy the food!

—Mario J. Porreca

A NOTE ON USING THIS BOOK

The front section of this book is titled "the Good;" this means that those recipes were designed with nutritional facts in mind, to help you eat food that is not only great tasting but also good for you. As professional chefs, taste was always the most important factor to Kirk and me, and therefore we created the second section to this book, "the Bad." This food is not bad! We live by the motto, "Progress, not perfection." So we believe there is room to eat some foods that are not all about the nutrition facts. We wanted to show you that it is OK to occasionally eat some foods that aren't the healthiest. The operative word is *occasionally*. Use these "bad" recipes as a reward for a significant number of days eating from the "good" recipes.

    I could never, ever diet. Especially being a chef, depriving myself constantly of the foods I love has never been a viable option for me. I was introduced to nutritional cleansing a couple of years ago, and utilizing that program allowed me to lose 70 pounds in five and a half months in a very healthy fashion while also allowing me to still occasionally enjoy the foods that I love. This not only allows me to stay on the program and stay the healthiest I have ever been, but it also takes away any guilt I would feel on a traditional diet. It works for me and has also worked for almost everyone I know who has cleansed. I'm not saying that you have to cleanse or that this book is useless without cleansing—not by any stretch. I'm simply saying that it has worked time and time again, so we did take that into consideration when designing these recipes. If you are cleansing, then these recipes are perfect for use with your program. If you aren't cleansing, then you can still enjoy and use these recipes to keep you on track for a healthy lifestyle. If you are not cleansing and would like to give it a shot while using this book, please check out our website at www.mariosmenu.com and click on the *Nutritional Cleansing* tab for more information.

    Thank you for taking the time to use this book. Not only do *we* thank you for it, but also we know that your taste buds and your health will thank you for it! Heck, the people for whom you prepare these recipes will also thank you! So thank you again, and please enjoy!

BASIC FACTS

Basic Knife Cuts

Strip Cuts

Batonnet: Translated from French, *batonnet* means "little stick." A batonnet cut measures ½ inch × ½ inch × 2½–3 inches. It is also the starting point for the medium dice.

Allumette: Also called the "matchstick cut," which is the French translation of *allumette*. The allumette measures ¼ inch × ¼ inch × 2½–3 inches. It is also the starting point for the small dice.

Julienne: It is often mistakenly thought that this cut is named for Julia Child, but the first reference to the julienne actually occurred in François Massialot's *Le Cuisinier Royal* in 1722, 190 years before Julia Child was even born. The julienne measures ⅛ inch × ⅛ inch × 2½ inches. It is also the starting point for the brunoise cut.

Fine Julienne: Measures 1/16 inch × 1/16 inch × 2 inches. It is also the starting point for the fine brunoise cut.

Cube Cuts

Large Dice: Cubes measuring ¾ inch × ¾ inch × ¾ inch.

Medium Dice: Cubes measuring ½ inch × ½ inch × ½ inch.

Small Dice: Cubes measuring ¼ inch × ¼ inch × ¼ inch and created by cutting the allumette cut into cubes.

Brunoise: Tiny cubes measuring ⅛ inch × ⅛ inch × ⅛ inch and created by cutting the julienne into cubes.

Fine Brunoise: Even tinier cubes, measuring 1/16 inch × 1/16 inch × 1/16 inch and created by cutting the fine julienne into cubes.

Slurry

A starch such as arrowroot, cornstarch, or potato starch dispersed in cold liquid to prevent it from forming lumps when added to hot liquid as a thickener.

Slurry will appear in some of the recipes in this book for thickening purposes. When referred to in this book, it is always slurry made from cornstarch and water. The ratio is ¼ teaspoon of cornstarch to 1½ ounces of water. When a recipe refers to 1 tablespoon of slurry, for example, it is understood that that means 1 tablespoon of cornstarch and water already combined following the proper ratio of ¼ teaspoon to 1½ ounce.

Temperatures and Descriptions of Degrees of Doneness

Degree of Doneness	Final Resting Temperature	Description
Fresh Beef, Veal, and Lamb		
Rare	135°F/57°C	Interior appearance shiny
Medium Rare	145°F/63°C	Deep red to pink
Medium	160°F/71°C	Pink to light pink
Well Done	170°F/77°C	Light pink with greying on the edges for medium well, and no pink for well done
Fresh Pork		
Medium	160°F/71°C	Meat opaque throughout, slight give, juices with faint blush
Well Done	170°F/77°C	Slight give, juices clear
Fresh Ham	160°F/71°C	Slight give, Juices with faint blush
Precooked (to reheat)	140°F/60°C	Meat already fully cooked
Poultry		
Whole Birds (chicken, turkey, duck, goose)	180°F/82°C	Leg easy to move in socket, juices with only blush
Poultry Breasts	170°F/77°C	Meat opaque, firm throughout
Poultry Thighs, Legs, Wings	180°F/82°C	Meat releases from bone
Stuffing (cooked alone or in bird)	165°F/74°C	
Ground Meat and Meat Mixtures		
Turkey, Chicken	165°F/74°C	Opaque throughout, juices clear
Beef, Veal, Lamb, Pork	160°F/71°C	Opaque, may have blush of red, juices opaque, no red
Seafood		
Fish	145°F/63°C	Still moist, separates easily into segments
Shrimp, Lobster, Crab		Shells turn red, flesh becomes pearly opaque
Scallops		Turn milky white or opaque and firm
Clams, Mussels, Oyster		Shells open

©The Professional Chef 8th Edition/The Culinary Institute of America

THE GOOD

Hors d'Oeuvre:
Any of various savory foods usually served as appetizers.

Hors d' oeuvres are fun! That is simply the first thing that comes to mind when I hear the word *hors d'oeuvre*. I think of foods that are passed around at parties or the beginning of a meal at a great restaurant. Hors d'oeuvres are the beginning, so it is only fitting that we begin our journey through this book with some fun hors d'oeuvre recipes.

When I think of a great hors d'oeuvre, I think of a flavor explosion in one bite. I also think of various textures and appealing colors. A first impression means everything, so it is very important that the hors d'oeuvres you prepare not only provide an exciting first impression but also leave your guests eagerly waiting to find out what's coming next. The hors d'oeuvres provide the buildup for the meal to come or can simply be passed around with a few cocktails throughout the night. Either way you choose to do it, it should be a lot of fun!

Although the term *hors d'oeuvre* is usually understood to mean anything served prior to a meal (as the definition from *Merriam-Webster's Collegiate Dictionary* at the beginning of this section reads), I tend to think of an hors d'oeuvre as different from an appetizer. An hors d'oeuvre is generally one or two bites and can be easily passed around at a party. An appetizer, on the other hand, is a small dish that should be enjoyed sitting at a table. An appetizer can be passed as well, but generally the entire plate is passed around a table for each guest to sample. The recipes you will find here are hors d'oeuvres in the sense that they can be easily passed and, aside from the dips, are prepared in individual one-bite portions.

We thought it was a great idea to include some dips in this section so that you can prepare them for different parties that you may host or take them with you to parties you may be attending. Dips are convenient because you don't have to spend as much time preparing them or as much attention to detail. You may also prepare dips a day ahead of time, store them in your refrigerator, and simply heat them in your oven before serving (assuming, of course, that it's a hot dip). Hors d'oeuvres are fun! Now use these recipes and go have some fun!

SECTION I

Hors d'Oeuvres

NUTRITION FACTS PER SERVING:

Calories: 225

Protein: 6g

Total Fat: 21g

Saturated Fat: 8g

Cholesterol: 37mg

Carbohydrates: 6g

Fiber: 1g

Sugars: 3g

Calcium: 84mg

Iron: 1mg

Grape Balls with Gorgonzola Cheese

Yield: 4 servings

1 ounce Gorgonzola cheese, crumbled

4 ounces cream cheese

2 ounces walnuts

12 each red grapes

PROCEDURE:

1. Microwave the crumbled Gorgonzola cheese on high for about 10 seconds, until just melted.
2. Thoroughly mix the melted Gorgonzola cheese with the cream cheese using a rubber spatula and refrigerate cheese mixture for at least 30 minutes before proceeding.
3. While the cheese mixture is in the refrigerator, coarsely chop the walnuts and place aside.
4. After the cheese mixture is thoroughly chilled, place the bowl with the cheese mixture into a slightly larger mixing bowl of ice to keep it cold.
5. Working quickly with dry hands, roll a thin layer of the cheese mixture around each red grape, coating it completely. If the cheese mixture begins to stick to your hands, simply wipe your hands clean with a dry towel and continue rolling.
6. Roll the coated grapes in the chopped walnuts just before serving. The grapes rolled in cheese can be stored in the refrigerator for up to 3 days before serving. *Do not roll in the walnuts until just before serving.*

NUTRITION FACTS PER SERVING:

Calories: 99

Protein: 7g

Total Fat: 5g

Saturated Fat: 2g

Cholesterol: 23mg

Carbohydrates: 6g

Fiber: 0g

Sugars: 6g

Calcium: 34mg

Iron: 0mg

Cajun Pork Tenderloin with Blue Cheese Honey Dipping Sauce

Yield: 6 servings

FOR THE PORK TENDERLOIN:

6 ounces pork tenderloin, cut into 1-ounce cubes

½ teaspoon extra virgin olive oil

1 tablespoon Paul Prudhomme's Meat Magic

1 tablespoon extra virgin olive oil

1 ounce blue cheese, crumbled

PROCEDURE:

1. In a mixing bowl, gently toss the cubes of pork tenderloin with ½ teaspoon of extra virgin olive oil and Paul Prudhomme's Meat Magic to coat evenly.
2. Preheat a small sauté pan over medium-high heat for 10-15 seconds. Then proceed by adding 1 tablespoon of extra virgin olive oil to the pan.
3. Sear the pork on all four sides and cook for about 4½ minutes or until the internal temperature of the pork has reached 160 degrees.
4. Allow the cooked pork to rest at room temperature for at least 5 minutes.
5. After resting, add a small crumble of blue cheese to the top of each cube of pork before skewering with a toothpick.

FOR THE BLUE CHEESE HONEY DIPPING SAUCE:

Yield: About 7 ounces of sauce

6 ounces honey

1 ounce blue cheese, crumbled

1 recipe Cajun pork tenderloin (see earlier recipe)

PROCEDURE:

1. In a small saucepan over medium heat, heat the honey until it just begins to thin out, about 30 seconds.
2. Add the crumbled blue cheese to the honey and whisk until all of the blue cheese has melted.
3. Remove the sauce from the pan and gently ladle onto a serving dish and place the skewered Cajun pork tenderloin directly onto the sauce.

NUTRITION FACTS PER SERVING:

Calories: 66

Protein: 3g

Total Fat: 5g

Saturated Fat: 3g

Cholesterol: 14mg

Carbohydrates: 2g

Fiber: 1g

Sugars: 1g

Calcium: 72mg

Iron: 1mg

Stuffed Crimini Mushrooms

Yield: 3 servings

6 crimini mushrooms
1 teaspoon extra virgin olive oil
1 ounce feta cheese, crumbled
1 teaspoon Parmesan cheese, grated
4 artichoke hearts, drained and roughly chopped
1 sun-dried tomato, roughly chopped
1 tablespoon raw spinach, chopped
Sea salt to taste
Ground white pepper to taste

PROCEDURE:

1. Remove the stems of the mushrooms and, using a teaspoon, gently scrape out the gills and discard.
2. Heat a small sauté pan over medium-high heat for about 10-15 seconds. Add the olive oil to the pan and begin sautéing the mushrooms for about 2 minutes on each side, until fork-tender.
3. Place mushrooms on a tray or dinner plate, stem side down (to release excess moisture) and refrigerate for at least 10 minutes.
4. In a small mixing bowl, combine the crumbled feta cheese, Parmesan cheese, chopped artichokes, chopped tomato, and chopped spinach. Season the filling with sea salt and ground white pepper and fold together with a rubber spatula.

    *Be sure to taste the filling before seasoning. Be careful with adding salt, because the Parmesan and feta cheeses already contain some salt.

5. Remove the mushrooms from the refrigerator and place them on a sprayed baking sheet, stem side up.
6. Place 1 teaspoon of filling into each mushroom cap.
7. Bake the filled mushrooms in a 350-degree oven for 10 minutes.
8. Serve immediately.

NUTRITION FACTS PER SERVING:

Calories: 36

Protein: 4g

Total Fat: 2g

Saturated Fat: 0g

Cholesterol: 17mg

Carbohydrates: 2g

Fiber: 1g

Sugars: 1g

Calcium: 23mg

Iron: 0mg

Crab and Avocado Salad

Yield: 12 servings of ½ stuffed cherry tomato each

8 ounces canned crabmeat, well drained

½ avocado, small dice

1 tablespoon dijon or whole-grain mustard

½ lemon, zest only

1 teaspoon sour cream

Sea salt to taste

Ground white pepper to taste

6 cherry tomatoes, halved and with seeds removed

1 tablespoon Paul Prudhomme's Seafood Magic

PROCEDURE:

1. Prepare the crabmeat salad by thoroughly combining the drained crabmeat, avocado, mustard, lemon zest, sour cream, salt, and pepper in a mixing bowl. Mix thoroughly and refrigerate.
2. Take the cherry tomatoes and cut them in half. Using a teaspoon, carefully remove the seeds from each half.
3. Place the Paul Prudhomme's Seafood Magic onto a dinner plate and dip each half of the seeded tomatoes into the Paul Prudhommes's Seafood Magic.
4. Evenly distribute the crabmeat salad into each tomato half.

NUTRITION FACTS PER SERVING:

Calories: 102

Protein: 3g

Total Fat: 6g

Saturated Fat: 1g

Cholesterol: 4mg

Carbohydrates: 9g

Fiber: 1g

Sugars: 1g

Calcium: 42mg

Iron: 1mg

Portobello Mushroom Bruschetta

Yield: 6 servings

6 ounces portobello mushrooms

1 tablespoon extra virgin olive oil

2 sprigs fresh thyme, flowers removed from stems and finely chopped

1 tablespoon mayonnaise

2 tablespoons Asiago cheese, grated

Sea salt to taste

Ground white pepper to taste

3 slices roasted garlic baguette (or French baguette), ½ inch thick, cut into halves

PROCEDURE:

1. Remove the stems from the mushrooms and discard. Using a teaspoon, gently scrape the gills from each mushroom and also discard. Small dice the mushroom caps.
2. Heat a small sauté pan over medium-high heat for 10-15 seconds, add the olive oil to the pan, and sauté the mushrooms for 2-3 minutes until fork-tender.
3. Place the sautéed mushrooms on a dinner plate and cool completely in the refrigerator.
4. In a mixing bowl, combine the cooled mushrooms, chopped thyme, mayonnaise, and Asiago cheese and thoroughly mix.
5. Season the mushroom mixture to taste with sea salt and ground white pepper.
6. Spoon 1 tablespoon of the mushroom mixture onto each half of the baguette, place on a clean baking sheet, and bake at 350 degrees for 8–10 minutes. The cheese should begin to melt and the mixture should be warm throughout.
7. Serve immediately.

NUTRITION FACTS PER SERVING:

Calories: 107

Protein: 6g

Total Fat: 2g

Saturated Fat: 1g

Cholesterol: 10mg

Carbohydrates: 15g

Fiber: 1g

Sugars: 0g

Calcium: 34mg

Iron: 1mg

King Crab and Brie Bruschetta

Yield: 6 servings

3 ounces king crabmeat

½ ounce Brie cheese, rind removed, small dice

1 teaspoon fresh chives, minced

1 teaspoon mayonnaise

Sea salt to taste

Ground white pepper to taste

6 slices baguette, ¼ inch thick

Drizzle of caramel sauce (from a jar) to garnish, if desired

PROCEDURE:

1. In a mixing bowl, combine the crabmeat, Brie, chives, and mayonnaise. Fold together to combine thoroughly and season to taste with sea salt and ground white pepper.
2. Spoon a mound of the crabmeat mixture onto each slice of baguette and bake on a baking sheet in a 350-degree oven for 5 to 7 minutes. The mixture should be warmed throughout, and the bread should be crisp on the outside.
3. Serve immediately. You may drizzle each piece lightly with caramel sauce to garnish, if desired.

NUTRITION FACTS PER SERVING:

Calories: 103

Protein: 6g

Total Fat: 8g

Saturated Fat: 2g

Cholesterol: 38mg

Carbohydrates: 2g

Fiber: 0g

Sugars: 1g

Calcium: 85mg

Iron: 1mg

Shrimp Scampi Dip

Yield: About 6 servings

4 ounces raw shrimp, tails removed

1 tablespoon extra virgin olive oil

1 tablespoon fresh basil, chopped

1 teaspoon garlic, minced

½ lemon, juice only

Pinch of sea salt

Pinch of ground white pepper

2 ounces pepperjack cheese, small dice

2 tablespoons celery, brunoise

1 tablespoon red onion, brunoise

1 tablespoon mayonnaise

½ tablespoon whole-grain mustard

6 tomato Triscuits, crushed

PROCEDURE:

1. In a mixing bowl, combine the shrimp, olive oil, chopped basil, garlic, and lemon juice. Season with sea salt and white pepper.
2. Heat a small sauté pan over medium-high heat for 10-15 seconds and sauté the marinated shrimp until they turn pink and are completely cooked.
3. Place the shrimp on a dinner plate and refrigerate until completely cooled.
4. Once they have cooled, proceed to small dice the shrimp and place them in a mixing bowl.
5. Add the pepperjack cheese, celery, red onion, mayonnaise, and mustard to the shrimp. Fold together until thoroughly combined.
6. Place the mixture in a small ovensafe crock and sprinkle the top with the crushed Triscuits to form a crust.
7. Cover the dip with foil and bake in a 350-degree oven for 10 minutes.
8. After 10 minutes, remove the foil and bake uncovered at 350 degrees for an additional 15 minutes or until crust becomes well browned and internal temperature reaches 150 degrees.
9. Remove from oven and serve immediately with your choice of bread or crackers.

NUTRITION FACTS PER SERVING:

Calories: 101

Protein: 6g

Total Fat: 7g

Saturated Fat: 2g

Cholesterol: 11mg

Carbohydrates: 4g

Fiber: 1g

Sugars: 2g

Calcium: 8mg

Iron: 1mg

Peanut Chicken Salad

Yield: About 10 servings of ½ tablespoon each

1 tablespoon extra virgin olive oil

6 ounces skinless, boneless chicken breast, small dice

2 ounces pineapple, small dice

1 red bell pepper, brunoise

2 ounces cashews

1 tablespoon mayonnaise

1 tablespoon organic peanut butter

1½ tablespoons coconut flakes

½ lime, juice only

½ teaspoon Sriracha (Asian hot chili sauce)

Sea salt to taste

Ground white pepper to taste

1 head romaine lettuce (to serve on)

PROCEDURE:

1. Heat a small sauté pan over medium-high heat for 10-15 seconds, add the olive oil to the pan, and begin sautéing the chicken.
2. As soon as the chicken begins to brown, add the pineapple, red bell pepper, and cashews to the pan and sauté until the chicken is thoroughly cooked (the chicken should reach an internal temperature of 165 degrees).
3. Place the mixture on a dinner plate and refrigerate until it is completely cooled.
4. Once the mixture is completely cooled, place in a mixing bowl and add the mayonnaise, peanut butter, coconut flakes, lime juice, Sriracha, sea salt, and white pepper and fold together to thoroughly combine.
5. Remove the outer leaves of the head of romaine and discard. Cut the inner leaves into spear shapes and serve salad on each leaf.

NUTRITION FACTS PER SERVING:

Calories: 87

Protein: 13g

Total Fat: 4g

Saturated Fat: 1g

Cholesterol: 34mg

Carbohydrates: 0g

Fiber: 0g

Sugars: 0g

Calcium: 79mg

Iron: 1mg

Turkey Saltimbocca with Basil Pesto Dipping Sauce

Yield: 5 servings

FOR THE BASIL PESTO DIPPING SAUCE:

2 teaspoons mayonnaise

1 teaspoon jarred basil pesto

PROCEDURE:

1. In a small mixing bowl, whisk together the mayonnaise and basil pesto until thoroughly combined.

FOR THE TURKEY SALTIMBOCCA:

5 slices of raw turkey breast, ¼ inch thick and 2 inches long

Pinch of ground white pepper

1¼ ounces Pecorino, sliced into 5 pieces of 1/4 ounce each, same size as the turkey

5 fresh sage leaves

5 slices prosciutto, sliced as thin as possible

Basil pesto dipping sauce to garnish (see earlier recipe)

PROCEDURE:

1. Lay the slices of turkey breast onto a cutting board and season each piece with a pinch of ground white pepper.
2. Place a slice of the Pecorino cheese on each slice of turkey so they are directly on top of one another, facing the same direction.
3. Place 1 sage leaf on top of each slice of Pecorino cheese.
4. Place each piece of turkey on one end of each piece of prosciutto and roll end to end, completely encasing turkey.
5. Heat a small nonstick sauté pan over medium-high heat for 10-15 seconds. Sear each turkey-prosciutto piece in a dry pan for 1-2 minutes on each side, until the prosciutto is crispy and the internal temperature of the turkey reaches 165 degrees.
6. Remove from pan and allow to rest at room temperature for 5 minutes.
7. Garnish with a dollop of basil pesto dipping sauce.

Breakfast:
The first meal of the day, especially when taken in the morning.

Breakfast really is the most important meal of the day. Everyone seems to know this fact, but very few people take it to heart. Breakfast is the most skipped meal of the day, and most of the time when people do eat breakfast, what they eat really isn't even considered a meal. Would you eat a banana or a cereal bar for dinner? So if breakfast is indeed so significant, then why is it not important to most people? It is my opinion that breakfast time is simply too early in the morning. Who wants to cook and clean up before having to spend all day at work? I know I don't!

I usually have a protein mineral shake for breakfast, which goes along with my nutritional cleansing program, but occasionally I do like to enjoy a big breakfast. Breakfast is actually my favorite meal. Whoever had the idea to serve breakfast in restaurants 24 hours a day is a genius. Honestly, the places that serve breakfast all day typically don't serve great food, but I will go there to eat because I know that no matter what time it is, I can have breakfast.

Another interesting thing about breakfast is that eating it can actually speed up your metabolism and help you to lose weight. Your metabolism is like a coal furnace: the furnace will not produce heat until you shovel coal into it. Your metabolism will not kick-start for the day until you put food in your body. Also keep in mind when you look at breakfast (as long as it is being eaten in the morning) that you don't have to be quite as calorie-conscious. I'm not telling you to go crazy and eat a 3,000-calorie breakfast. I'm simply saying that if there is a meal where your calorie count can be a bit more flexible, it's breakfast. The reason for this is that you are eating it first thing to start your day, so everything you do until you go to sleep will be burning those calories. Breakfast truly is the most important meal of the day and can be infinitely beneficial for you. We have included these recipes in hopes of getting you started on a healthy lifestyle that includes enjoying breakfast every day.

SECTION II

Breakfast

NUTRITION FACTS PER SERVING:

Calories: 146

Protein: 4g

Total Fat: 1g

Saturated Fat: 0g

Cholesterol: 0mg

Carbohydrates: 30g

Fiber: 2g

Sugars: 4g

Calcium: 19mg

Iron: 1mg

Whole-Grain Breakfast Porridge

Yield: 8 servings of about 4 ounces each

½ cup brown rice

½ cup steel-cut oats

¼ cup barley

½ cup Cream of Wheat cereal

1 teaspoon cinnamon

¼ teaspoon nutmeg

¼ teaspoon ground ginger

2 star anise

5 cups water (or rice milk for richer porridge)

1 teaspoon vanilla extract

2 tablespoons light agave nectar

1 tablespoon light brown sugar (per serving) to garnish

1 tablespoon chopped walnuts (per serving) to garnish

Dash of cinnamon (per serving) to garnish

1 strawberry (per serving) to garnish

*Agave nectar is an all-natural sweetener that is similar to honey and is very low on the glycemic index. Agave nectar can be found at most major supermarkets.

PROCEDURE:

1. Combine brown rice, oats, barley, Cream of Wheat, cinnamon, nutmeg, ginger, star anise, water, and vanilla extract in a rice cooker. Depending on your rice cooker, you may need to set to either *porridge* setting or cook for 45–50 minutes.
2. Stir when finished to thoroughly combine the porridge.
3. Remove the star anise and discard.
4. Stir in the agave nectar to combine thoroughly.
5. Spoon into bowls and garnish each bowl with a sprinkling of brown sugar, chopped walnuts, cinnamon, and a strawberry if desired.

*Porridge can be made up to 12 hours ahead of time and kept warm in your rice cooker on the *warm* setting.

Stuffed French Toast with Blueberry Honey

Yield: 6 servings of 1 slice each

FOR THE FILLING:

1 medium strawberry with stem removed, quartered

4 mandarin orange segments

¼ teaspoon vanilla extract

4 ounces Mascarpone cheese

½ orange, zest only

1 teaspoon honey

PROCEDURE:

1. In a food processor, puree the strawberry, mandarin orange segments, and vanilla extract until smooth.
2. In a mixing bowl, combine the fruit puree (from above), Mascarpone cheese, orange zest, and honey.
3. Cover with plastic wrap and refrigerate for at least 30 minutes before using.

FOR THE BLUEBERRY HONEY:

¼ cup honey

¼ cup light agave nectar

¼ cup fresh blueberries

PROCEDURE:

1. In a saucepan over medium heat, combine all ingredients.
2. When the blueberries pop and the honey becomes a pink or magenta color, remove from heat and strain through a mesh strainer.
3. Reserve sauce.

FOR THE STUFFED FRENCH TOAST:

3 eggs

¼ teaspoon cinnamon

Pinch of nutmeg

¼ teaspoon vanilla extract

½ cup almond milk

6 2-ounce slices multigrain bread

1 recipe French toast filling (see earlier recipe)

1 recipe blueberry honey (see earlier recipe)

Fresh blueberries and raspberries to garnish

PROCEDURE:

1. In a mixing bowl, whisk eggs, cinnamon, nutmeg, vanilla extract, and almond milk until thoroughly combined.
2. Pour egg mixture into a shallow baking pan and reserve.
3. Insert a paring knife into the bottom of the crust of the multigrain bread. Using a back-and-forth motion, make a small pocket without puncturing either side of the bread.
4. Place the French toast filling into a piping bag. Insert the tip of the piping bag into the pocket of the bread and pipe filling until the pocket is full but not pouring out.
5. Proceed by dipping each piece of filled bread into the egg mixture, making sure both sides are completely coated.
6. Brown the French toast on both sides on either a sprayed griddle or in a sprayed nonstick sauté pan over medium heat until golden brown on each side.
7. Place the browned French toast onto a sprayed baking sheet and bake in a 350-degree oven for about 10 minutes. The French toast should be warm throughout but should not get much darker in the oven. The internal temperature of the French toast should reach at least 150 degrees.
8. Place the French toast onto plates or a serving tray and drizzle with the blueberry honey. Garnish the plates or tray with fresh blueberries and raspberries. Serve hot, so that the filling oozes when the French toast is cut.

STUFFED FRENCH TOAST WITH BLUEBERRY HONEY

NUTRITION FACTS PER SERVING:

Calories: 193

Protein: 6g

Total Fat: 15g

Saturated Fat: 5g

Cholesterol: 91mg

Carbohydrates: 10g

Fiber: 1g

Sugars: 8g

Calcium: 49mg

Iron: 1mg

NUTRITION FACTS PER SERVING:

Calories: 241

Protein: 16g

Total Fat: 16g

Saturated Fat: 6g

Cholesterol: 250mg

Carbohydrates: 8g

Fiber: 1g

Sugars: 7g

Calcium: 136mg

Iron: 2mg

Breakfast Casserole

Yield: 9 servings

6 links turkey breakfast sausage, roughly chopped

6 slices uncured bacon, small dice

1 tablespoon Paul Prudhomme's Meat Magic

25 asparagus tips

9 eggs

1½ cups organic whole milk

2 tablespoons chives, snipped

2 ounces Provolone cheese, shredded

Watermelon and fresh berries to garnish

PROCEDURE:

1. In a sauté pan, slowly render the sausage and bacon over medium heat until browned.
2. Season the sausage and bacon with Paul Prudhomme's Meat Magic and add the asparagus tips to the pan. Cook for an additional 2 minutes, then transfer mixture to a dinner plate and chill in refrigerator.
3. In a mixing bowl, add eggs, milk, and chives and whisk until thoroughly combined.
4. Spread the meat mixture evenly on the bottom of a sprayed 9"x9" baking pan.
5. Pour the egg mixture over the meat mixture in the pan and sprinkle the top with the Provolone cheese.
6. Cover the pan with aluminum foil and bake in a 325-degree oven for 30–35 minutes or until the egg is firm and set completely.
7. Allow the casserole to rest at room temperature for at least 10 minutes before cutting.
8. Cut the casserole into 9 equal-sized squares, garnish with watermelon and fresh berries, and serve immediately.

Steak and Eggs with Asiago Cream Sauce

Yield: 6 servings

FOR THE ASIAGO CREAM SAUCE:

1 cup organic whole milk

Sea salt to taste

Ground white pepper to taste

1 teaspoon garlic powder

2 tablespoons slurry

2 tablespoons grated Asiago cheese

NUTRITION FACTS PER SERVING:

Calories: 387

Protein: 23g

Total Fat: 24g

Saturated Fat: 6g

Cholesterol: 252mg

Carbohydrates: 19g

Fiber: 1g

Sugars: 2g

Calcium: 123mg

Iron: 3mg

PROCEDURE:

1. In a saucepan, combine the milk, salt, white pepper, and garlic powder and bring to a boil over medium heat.
2. Add the slurry to the sauce to thicken and bring back to a boil while continuously whisking.
3. Add the Asiago cheese to the sauce.
4. Allow sauce to cook an additional 2 minutes and remove from heat.
5. Cover and reserve.

STEAK AND EGGS:

6 slices roasted garlic baguette (French baguette can be substituted), ¼ inch thick
2 tablespoons extra virgin olive oil
Sea salt to taste
Ground white pepper to taste
6 2-ounce pieces filet mignon
5 cups water
3 tablespoons white vinegar
6 eggs
Asiago cream sauce (see earlier recipe)
3 tablespoons salsa to garnish, strained to remove liquid (discard liquid)

PROCEDURE:

1. Brush the bread with a thin layer of extra virgin olive oil, season with salt and pepper, and grill on both sides until both sides have grill marks.
2. Brush the filet mignon with extra virgin olive oil, season with salt and pepper, and grill for about 2 minutes on each side, until medium rare.
3. While the steak is cooking, combine water, a pinch of salt, and the vinegar and bring to a boil.
4. Turn the water down until the boiling subsides and, using a slotted spoon, stir the water in a swirling motion.
5. Crack each egg into individual containers and allow each egg to slide into the center of the swirling water and poach for 90 seconds.
6. After 90 seconds, remove the eggs from the water with the slotted spoon.
7. Place a piece of grilled bread in the center of the plate, place a filet on top of the bread, place a poached egg on top of the filet, season the egg with salt and pepper, spoon 2-4 tablespoons of sauce over the egg, and spoon ½ tablespoon of the strained salsa onto the top of each to garnish. Serve immediately.

NUTRITION FACTS PER SERVING:

Calories: 308

Protein: 21g

Total Fat: 17g

Saturated Fat: 4g

Cholesterol: 437mg

Carbohydrates: 19g

Fiber: 3g

Sugars: 13g

Calcium: 82mg

Iron: 3mg

Chicken and Sun-Dried Tomato Omelet

Yield: 1 Serving of 1 omelet

1 teaspoon extra virgin olive oil
2 sun-dried tomatoes, fine julienne
1 scallion, finely chopped
1 ounce chicken, canned
2 eggs
1 tablespoon water
Sea salt to taste
Ground white pepper to taste
½ teaspoon Italian seasoning
1 tablespoon grated Asiago cheese

PROCEDURE:
1. Heat a small nonstick omelet pan over medium-low heat for 10-15 seconds; add the olive oil, sun-dried tomatoes, scallion, and chicken. Sauté until just warmed through.
2. In a mixing bowl, whisk the eggs, water, salt, pepper, and Italian seasoning until thoroughly combined and bubbles begin to form (you may do this in a blender for a lighter omelet).
3. When the chicken mixture is warmed through, spray the pan (with the chicken, tomatoes, and scallion still in it) with nonstick cooking spray.
4. Pour the egg mixture into the center of the pan and allow it to spread through the pan evenly.
5. Using a rubber spatula, keep pulling the egg away from the sides of the pan to avoid sticking and to also allow more egg to fill in the sides of the pan.
6. Once the egg is almost set, flip the omelet so that the other side can cook for about 1 minute.
7. Sprinkle the grated Asiago cheese onto the omelet, fold it in half with your rubber spatula, and serve immediately.

Soup:
A liquid food, especially with a meat, fish, or vegetable stock as a base and often containing pieces of solid food.

Let's talk about soup! I love soup! Most of us love soup! It's almost a universal law. From a child loving alphabet soup to an adult anxiously awaiting the melty cheesy goodness of a piping-hot crock of French onion soup, we all have a connection with soup. If you're sick, all you want is a bowl of Mom's chicken noodle soup. If it's cold outside…well, you get the idea! Almost anything that happens can either be fixed or enhanced with a great bowl of soup. A meal can start with soup, consist of just the soup itself, or end with a great fruit or, yes, even chocolate soup!

It's hard to think of a more versatile or comforting food to have on the table. Even great television is quick to point out this fact. Take *Seinfeld* for instance: everyone knows who the Soup Nazi is. Why not the Salad Nazi or the Dessert Nazi? The answer is simple: soup is just more fun! Yes, I said it! Soup is more fun than dessert! It certainly can make you feel just as good, with a lot of the dessert-like effects being avoided. Not to say that dessert is bad at all, but a great bowl of soup can be better!

When tackling soup for this book, we wanted to show you that you do not have to slave over a hot stove all day to get what you are craving. The bowl of soup that you have been looking for can be done quickly and easily and still taste just as good as, if not better than, you are expecting. So let's have some soup! Keep in mind that soup also goes great with the upcoming sections in this book. Feel free to mix and match the different soups, salads, and sandwiches to make a great meal. Or simply enjoy these soups as a meal all on their own. Either way, please have fun and enjoy some great soup!

SECTION III

Soup

NUTRITION FACTS PER SERVING:

Calories: 102

Protein: 4g

Total Fat: 0g

Saturated Fat: 0g

Cholesterol: 2mg

Carbohydrates: 23g

Fiber: 2g

Sugars: 15g

Calcium: 128mg

Iron: 0mg

Chilled Strawberry, Banana, and Vanilla Bean Soup

Yield: 4 servings of 4 ounces (½ cup) each

6 medium-sized strawberries with tops removed, roughly chopped

½ vanilla bean, split and scraped (or ¼ teaspoon pure vanilla extract)

2 6-ounce containers vanilla yogurt

2 bananas, roughly chopped

1 strawberry, sliced (per serving to garnish)

⅛ banana, small dice (per serving to garnish)

PROCEDURE:

1. In a blender, combine the strawberries, vanilla, yogurt, and bananas and puree until smooth.
2. Transfer chilled soup into a lidded container and refrigerate for at least 1 hour before serving.
3. Garnish with a sliced strawberry and diced banana.

*Soup may be made up to a day ahead of time.

NUTRITION FACTS PER SERVING:

Calories: 158

Protein: 5g

Total Fat: 11g

Saturated Fat: 5g

Cholesterol: 25mg

Carbohydrates: 11g

Fiber: 2g

Sugars: 5g

Calcium: 167mg

Iron: 1mg

Red Bell Pepper Soup

Yield: 6 servings of 4 ounces (½ cup) each

2 tablespoons extra virgin olive oil

2 leeks with first 2 outer layers peeled off, roughly chopped

1 stalk of celery, roughly chopped

3 medium red bell peppers with core and stem removed, roughly chopped

½ white onion, peeled and roughly chopped

1 bay leaf

1 tablespoon all-purpose flour

16 ounces organic vegetable stock

Sea salt to taste

Ground white pepper to taste

6 ounces Feta cheese, crumbled (to garnish)

6 tablespoons fresh chives, minced (to garnish)

PROCEDURE:

1. Add the 2 tablespoons of extra virgin olive oil to a soup pot over high heat. Sweat the leeks, celery, red peppers, onion, and bay leaf for 5 minutes.
2. After 5 minutes on high heat, reduce the heat to medium and allow to cook for 10 minutes on medium heat. Be sure to stir occasionally to avoid sticking or burning.
3. After the vegetables have cooked for the additional 10 minutes, mix in 1 tablespoon of flour and allow flour to cook for about 30 seconds.
4. Add the 16 ounces of vegetable stock and cook for an additional 5 minutes while stirring occasionally. Total cooking time is 20 minutes.
5. After cooking for the final 5 minutes, discard the bay leaf and carefully transfer the contents to a blender. Make sure the lid is securely placed onto the blender. Using a kitchen towel, cover the lid of the blender and use your hand to keep pressure on the lid while blending. Puree the soup about 2 or 3 minutes, until it is completely smooth. If the soup seems a bit thick, blend in some additional vegetable stock or water.
6. Season to taste with sea salt and ground white pepper and garnish with crumbled Feta cheese and fresh chives. Serve hot.

NUTRITION FACTS PER SERVING:

Calories: 189

Protein: 4g

Total Fat: 12g

Saturated Fat: 1g

Cholesterol: 0mg

Carbohydrates: 19g

Fiber: 4g

Sugars: 10g

Calcium: 59mg

Iron: 1mg

Pear and Parsnip Bisque

Yield: 8 servings of 4 ounces (½ cup) each

3 tablespoons extra virgin olive oil

2 small shallots, roughly chopped

½ medium onion, peeled and roughly chopped

1 leek, roughly chopped (discard the dark green leaves)

2 parsnips, peeled and roughly chopped

1 bay leaf

10 whole white peppercorns

2 d'Anjou pears, peeled and roughly chopped

1 stalk of celery, roughly chopped

3 sprigs of fresh thyme

4 cups organic vegetable stock

1 teaspoon cinnamon

¼ teaspoon Nutmeg

8 ounces vanilla-flavored almond milk

2 tablespoons honey

Dash of cayenne

Allspice to taste

Sea salt to taste

Ground white pepper to taste

PROCEDURE:

1. In a soup pot over medium-high heat, add the olive oil and slowly begin to caramelize the shallots, onion, leek, parsnips, bay leaf, peppercorns, pears, celery, and thyme. This will take roughly 25 minutes. Be sure to stir regularly.
2. After the vegetables are caramelized, add the 4 cups of vegetable stock to the pan and bring to a boil.
3. Once soup comes to a boil, reduce heat and simmer for 25 minutes.
4. Remove the bay leaf and thyme sprigs and carefully transfer the contents to a blender. Make sure the lid is securely placed onto the blender. Using a kitchen towel, cover the lid of the blender and use your hand to keep pressure on the lid while blending. Puree the soup about 2 or 3 minutes, until it is completely smooth.
5. Season with cinnamon and nutmeg. Turn blender on low speed and slowly incorporate the almond milk, honey, cayenne, allspice, sea salt, and white pepper to taste.
6. Serve hot.

NUTRITION FACTS PER SERVING:

Calories: 242

Protein: 7g

Total Fat: 10g

Saturated Fat: 3g

Cholesterol: 0mg

Carbohydrates: 19g

Fiber: 2g

Sugars: 6g

Calcium: 123mg

Iron: 2mg

Sweet 5-Onion Soup with Gruyere Cheese Croustade

Yield: 5 servings of 4 ounces (½ cup) each

FOR THE GRUYERE CHEESE CROUSTADE:
2 tablespoons extra virgin olive oil
5 slices whole-grain baguette, sliced ¼ inch thick on a bias
1 ounce Gruyere cheese, sliced thin
3 sprigs fresh thyme, leaves only, finely chopped

PROCEDURE:
1. Using a pastry brush, brush a thin layer of olive oil on one side of each of the sliced whole-grain baguettes.
2. Place a slice of Gruyere cheese on each piece of baguette.
3. Sprinkle the chopped thyme on top of each piece of cheese.
4. Bake on an ungreased baking sheet at 350 degrees for 15 minutes.
5. Serve 1 croustade with each serving of soup.

FOR THE SWEET 5-ONION SOUP:
1 large white onion, peeled and sliced
1 medium red onion, peeled and sliced
6 regular shallots, peeled and sliced
6 tablespoons scallions, green part only, chopped
2 medium leeks, roughly chopped (discard the dark green leaves)
1 tablespoon organic butter
½ cup Jack Daniel's whiskey
4 cups beef stock
Sea salt to taste
Cracked black pepper to taste
1 recipe Gruyere cheese croustade (see earlier recipe)

PROCEDURE:
1. In a soup pot over medium heat, add the onions and then add the butter.
2. Occasionally stir the onions while they caramelize so they do not stick to the bottom of the pot. This process will take about 40 minutes.
3. Once the onions are caramelized, add the Jack Daniel's to the pan while stirring to deglaze the pan. Continue cooking for an additional 10 minutes or until liquid reduces by half.
4. Add the beef stock, bring to a boil, season with sea salt and cracked black pepper to taste, and serve with a Gruyere cheese croustade.

NUTRITION FACTS PER SERVING:

Calories: 205

Protein: 12g

Total Fat: 7g

Saturated Fat: 1g

Cholesterol: 10mg

Carbohydrates: 25g

Fiber: 5g

Sugars: 6g

Calcium: 72mg

Iron: 2mg

Wild Mushroom and White Bean Soup

Yield: 6 servings of 4 ounces (½ cup) each

3 tablespoons extra virgin olive oil

1 large leek, roughly chopped (discard the dark green leaves)

1 large onion, peeled and roughly chopped

1 medium shallot, peeled and roughly chopped

1 ounce dried wild mushrooms

2 sprigs fresh thyme

2 chicken sausage links (basil and sun-dried tomato flavored), 1 link roughly chopped and 1 link reserved, sliced into 10 even slices for garnish

1 15-ounce can cannellini beans divided in half, half for soup and half for garnish

4 cups organic chicken stock

Sea salt to taste

Ground white pepper to taste

6 ounces baby spinach, julienne (for garnish)

PROCEDURE:

1. In a soup pot over medium heat, add the olive oil and sauté the leeks, onions, shallots, dried mushrooms, thyme, chopped chicken sausage, and half of the beans for 5–10 minutes or until they begin to stick to the pot.
2. Add the chicken stock and simmer for 25 minutes.
3. Remove the sprigs of thyme and discard.
4. Carefully transfer the soup to a blender. Make sure the lid is securely placed onto the blender. Using a kitchen towel, cover the lid of the blender and use your hand to keep pressure on the lid while blending. Puree the soup about 2 or 3 minutes, until it is completely smooth. Season to taste with salt and ground white pepper.
5. In a dry nonstick sauté pan, brown the reserved slices of chicken sausage on both sides.
6. Garnish with the browned chicken sausage, reserved cannellini beans, and julienne of fresh spinach.

NUTRITION FACTS PER SERVING:

Calories: 135

Protein: 12g

Total Fat: 4g

Saturated Fat: 1g

Cholesterol: 36mg

Carbohydrates: 14g

Fiber: 3g

Sugars: 4g

Calcium: 69mg

Iron: 2mg

Chilled Seafood Gazpacho

Yield: 5 servings of 4 ounces (½ cup) each

5 ounces zucchini, small dice

4 ounces yellow squash, small dice

1 small shallot, peeled, small dice

½ large red onion, peeled, small dice

1 teaspoon garlic, peeled and chopped

1 14.5-ounce can diced tomatoes

2 tablespoons white wine vinegar

Dash of sea salt

Dash of ground white pepper

Dash of smoked paprika

Dash of celery salt

½ cup spicy bloody mary mix

3 ounces raw 51/60 shrimp, tails removed

3 ounces bay scallops

1 each sea scallop to garnish

1 tablespoon extra virgin olive oil

½ tablespoon Old Bay seasoning

½ can black beans (to garnish)

2 tablespoons scallions, chopped (to garnish)

PROCEDURE:

1. In a blender, puree the zucchini, squash, shallot, red onion, garlic, diced tomatoes, vinegar, sea salt, white pepper, smoked paprika, celery salt, and bloody mary mix. Reserve and place in the refrigerator, covered.
2. While soup is chilling, in a mixing bowl, toss the shrimp and both scallops with the olive oil and Old Bay seasoning.
3. In a dry sauté pan over medium-high heat, sauté the seasoned shrimp and bay scallops until fully cooked.
4. Transfer the cooked seafood from the pan onto a dinner plate and place in the refrigerator until fully chilled.
5. While the seafood is chilling, sear the sea scallops in a sauté pan over high heat on both sides for about 3-4 minutes per side. The scallops should be caramelized on both sides and the center should be slightly firm to the touch. Set the cooked sea scallops aside to use as a garnish.
6. Combine the chilled shrimp and bay scallops with the chilled soup, prepared earlier, and blend until smooth.
7. Serve chilled and garnished with the cooked sea scallops, black beans, and chopped scallions.

Salad:
Any of various usually cold dishes as
    a). Raw greens (as lettuce) often combined with other vegetables and toppings and served, especially with dressing.
    b). Small pieces of food (as pasta, meat, fruit, or vegetables) usually mixed with a dressing (as mayonnaise) or set in gelatin.

Salads are the quintessential health food in most people's mind. The number one complaint heard from people on a diet or trying to get healthier is, "I'm so tired of eating salads!" It's easy to see how you can get tired of eating the same food day in and day out, especially if you're not really sure how to make that food taste really good in the first place.

    As you can see from the definition above, salads are very versatile. You can do almost anything with a salad. You just have to know what you like and how you like it. This can be a daunting task when it comes to salads, because you have so many options about so many different things! For example, you get to choose from many different readily available lettuces, vegetables, proteins, toppings, and, of course, everybody's favorite, dressings. So I guess you could say building a salad for yourself can be more complicated than most people's wardrobe.

    So how do you do it? Excellent question, and the answer is simple: you try things. You try different things over and over until you have found exactly what it is you are looking for, along the way giving yourself viable options for new ideas to keep things fresh and fun. In my opinion, salads should not be an everyday food, other than a side salad as an accompaniment to a larger meal. The side salad is an easy one; it's almost like the cousin of the entrée salads we are talking about here. Don't be nervous, though; feel free to scale down any of the recipes in this section to transform them into a nice side-salad accompaniment. Also, feel free to mix and match the ingredients and dressings provided in this section. If you like something different, then by all means go for it!

    One thing I will tell you is that if there is one thing you take from this section, make it the dressings. Store-bought premade salad dressings are really not very conducive to good health. Aside from the chemicals that are in a lot of them, *low fat* on a label usually means high sugar. So the dressings in this section are a great thing to really use often. This is an important section in this book. Salads represent a big part of "the Good" when it comes to eating cleaner. So please, enjoy these salads!

*Dressing recipes have been designed in some cases to yield more than the salad recipes. Most salad dressings can be made in larger quantities and stored in the refrigerator for later use.

SECTION IV

Salads

Strawberry Fennel Salad with White Balsamic Vinaigrette

FOR THE WHITE BALSAMIC VINAIGRETTE

Yield: 4 servings of 2 ounces each

1 tablespoon honey
3 tablespoons white balsamic vinegar
4 tablespoons extra virgin olive oil
Sea salt to taste
Ground white pepper to taste

PROCEDURE:
1. Combine the honey and vinegar in a mixing bowl.
2. Whisking slowly, drizzle the extra virgin olive oil into the honey and vinegar mixture.
3. Season to taste with sea salt and ground white pepper.

STRAWBERRY FENNEL SALAD WITH WHITE BALSAMIC VINAIGRETTE

Yield: 1 serving

1 ounce baby spinach, washed and drained
1 ounce baby arugula, washed and drained
¼ bulb fennel, cored and sliced thin
2 ounces white balsamic vinaigrette (see earlier recipe)
½ cup mandarin orange segments, drained
3 medium-sized strawberries with tops removed, sliced
1 ounce slivered almonds
1 ounce goat cheese, crumbled
Sea salt to taste
Fresh cracked black pepper to taste

PROCEDURE:

1. Toss the spinach, arugula, and fennel in a mixing bowl with 1 ounce of the white balsamic dressing.
2. Place the dressed salad onto a serving plate and garnish with mandarin oranges, sliced strawberries, slivered almonds, and crumbled goat cheese. Drizzle salad with 1 ounce additional white balsamic dressing.
3. Season to taste with sea salt and cracked black pepper and serve immediately.

NUTRITION FACTS PER SERVING (DRESSING ONLY):

Calories: 138

Protein: 0g

Total Fat: 14g

Saturated Fat: 2g

Cholesterol: 0mg

Carbohydrates: 4g

Fiber: 0g

Sugars: 4g

Calcium: 2mg

Iron: 0mg

NUTRITION FACTS PER SERVING (SALAD ONLY):

Calories: 360

Protein: 17g

Total Fat: 25g

Saturated Fat: 8g

Cholesterol: 29mg

Carbohydrates: 22g

Fiber: 7g

Sugars: 12g

Calcium: 425 mg

Iron: 4mg

STRAWBERRY FENNEL SALAD WITH WHITE BALSAMIC VINAIGRETTE

Grilled Romaine Salad with Whole-Wheat Croustade and Creamy Avocado-Lemon Dressing

FOR THE CREAMY AVOCADO-LEMON DRESSING:
Yield: 3 servings

1 tablespoon mayonnaise
1 teaspoon fat-free sour cream
½ lemon, zest and juice
¼ avocado, peeled
1 tablespoon water
Sea salt to taste
Ground white pepper to taste

PROCEDURE:
1. In a mixing bowl, combine the mayonnaise, sour cream, lemon zest, and lemon juice and whisk until thoroughly mixed.
2. Take the avocado and place it on a cutting board. Using the side of your knife, mash it back and forth until it is a relatively smooth puree.
3. Whisk the avocado puree into the mayonnaise mixture and adjust the consistency with about 1 tablespoon of water. The dressing should be about the consistency of traditional ranch dressing.
4. Season with sea salt and ground white pepper to taste.

FOR THE CROUSTADE:
1 slice whole-wheat bread (will yield 3 croustades)
1 teaspoon extra virgin olive oil
1 teaspoon Parmesan cheese, grated

PROCEDURE:
1. Remove crust from wheat bread and cut into three equal rectangular shapes.
2. Using a pastry brush, brush each rectangle with a thin layer of extra virgin olive oil.

3. Sprinkle each piece of coated bread with a thin layer of Parmesan cheese.
4. Bake in either a toaster oven on *toast* setting or a 350-degree oven for about 3–4 minutes. The croustade should be browned on the top and crisp on the outside. If the middle is still soft to the touch, allow it to cool at room temperature, and it will become crispy throughout.

FOR THE SALAD:

3 heads of romaine lettuce, tops trimmed and cut in half lengthwise

3 slices red onion, about ¼ inch thick

1 tablespoon extra virgin olive oil

3 slices yellow heirloom tomato, about ¼ inch thick

9 cherry tomatoes

3 whole-wheat croustades (see earlier recipe)

1 recipe creamy avocado-lemon dressing (see earlier recipe)

PROCEDURE:

1. Lightly rub each half of the romaine head and the slices of red onion with extra virgin olive oil. Grill the inner side of the Romaine for about 2 minutes and the slices of red onion for about 3 minutes.
2. Arrange all of the salad ingredients on a serving plate; you may do it as the picture shows or to your desired preference.
3. Drizzle the composed salad with the creamy avocado-lemon dressing and serve immediately.

*The beauty of this salad is that it is very versatile. While most of the ingredients are raw, the romaine and the onion are grilled. The romaine should be grilled just before serving and served immediately, while the onion may be done in advance and even served chilled if you would like. You may also season the slice of tomato with sea salt and fresh cracked black pepper.

NUTRITION FACTS PER SERVING (DRESSING ONLY):

Calories: 96

Protein: 1g

Total Fat: 10g

Saturated Fat: 1g

Cholesterol: 6mg

Carbohydrates: 3g

Fiber: 1g

Sugars: 0g

Calcium: 7mg

Iron: 0mg

NUTRITION FACTS PER SERVING (SALAD AND CROUSTADE ONLY):

Calories: 197

Protein: 9g

Total Fat: 9g

Saturated Fat: 1g

Cholesterol: 1mg

Carbohydrates: 26g

Fiber: 14g

Sugars: 10g

Calcium: 233mg

Iron: 6mg

GRILLED ROMAINE SALAD WITH WHOLE-WHEAT CROUSTADE AND CREAMY AVOCADO-LEMON DRESSING

Roasted Chicken and Apple Salad with Pomegranate–Poppy Seed Vinaigrette

FOR THE POMEGRANATE–POPPY SEED VINAIGRETTE:
Yield: 3 servings of 2 ounces each

2 tablespoons poppy seeds
3 tablespoons pomegranate juice
2 tablespoons raspberry vinegar
1 tablespoon honey
1 lemon, juice only
4 tablespoons extra virgin olive oil
Sea salt to taste
Ground white pepper to taste

PROCEDURE:
1. In a small, dry sauté pan over medium heat, toast the poppy seeds, stirring constantly until they begin to smell nutty.
2. In a blender, combine the toasted poppy seeds, pomegranate juice, raspberry vinegar, honey, and lemon juice.
3. Blend on medium-low speed with no lid on the blender, and slowly drizzle in the olive oil to combine.
4. Season to taste with sea salt and ground white pepper.

FOR THE SALAD:
Yield: 1 serving

1 6-ounce chicken breast
½ lemon, zest only
½ teaspoon fresh thyme leaves, roughly chopped
½ teaspoon fresh rosemary, leaves only, roughly chopped
Pinch of sea salt
Pinch of ground white pepper
1 tablespoon extra virgin olive oil

1 ounce baby spinach, stems removed

1 ounce baby romaine lettuce, red and green

⅛ Granny Smith apple, outside only, fine julienne

⅛ Fuji apple, outside only, fine julienne

1 sun-dried tomato, fine julienne

½ ounce pecans, halved

1 ounce cranberry Stilton cheese, crumbled

2 ounces pomegranate–poppy seed vinaigrette (see earlier recipe)

PROCEDURE:

1. Rub the chicken breast with the lemon zest, thyme, and rosemary on each side. Season the chicken with a pinch of sea salt and ground white pepper.
2. Heat a small sauté pan over medium-high heat for 10–15 seconds, add the olive oil, and sear each side of the chicken until brown.
3. Place the seared chicken on a sprayed sheet pan and roast at 350 degrees for about 10 minutes, until the internal temperature of the chicken reaches 165 degrees.
4. Allow the chicken to rest for at least 10 minutes at room temperature before dicing.
5. Large dice the roasted chicken breast.
6. Toss together the spinach, romaine, apples, sun-dried tomato, pecans, Stilton cheese, and 1 ounce of the pomegranate–poppy seed vinaigrette.
7. Place the salad on a serving plate and place the diced chicken on top of the salad. Drizzle with an additional 1 ounce of the pomegranate–poppy seed vinaigrette and serve.

NUTRITION FACTS PER SERVING (DRESSING ONLY):

Calories: 111

Protein: 1g

Total Fat: 10g

Saturated Fat: 1g

Cholesterol: 0mg

Carbohydrates: 5g

Fiber: 0g

Sugars: 4g

Calcium: 44mg

Iron: 0mg

NUTRITION FACTS PER SERVING (SALAD ONLY):

Calories: 445

Protein: 41g

Total Fat: 27g

Saturated Fat: 8g

Cholesterol: 102mg

Carbohydrates: 11g

Fiber: 3g

Sugars: 6g

Calcium: 218mg

Iron: 3mg

ROASTED CHICKEN AND APPLE SALAD WITH POMEGRANATE–POPPY SEED VINAIGRETTE

SALADS 61

Pittsburgh Steak Salad with Scallion Buttermilk Ranch Dressing

FOR THE SCALLION BUTTERMILK RANCH DRESSING:
Yield: 3 servings of 1 ⅓ tablespoons each

2 scallions, root removed and discarded
1 ounce spinach
3 tablespoons fat-free sour cream
1 tablespoon ranch seasoning mix from packet
1 lime, zest and juice
5 tablespoons low-fat buttermilk
Pinch of celery salt
Sea salt to taste
Ground white pepper to taste

PROCEDURE:
1. In a blender, puree the scallions, spinach, sour cream, ranch seasoning, lime zest, and lime juice until smooth.
2. Transfer the puree from the blender to a mixing bowl and whisk in the buttermilk to incorporate it into the puree.
3. Season with a pinch of celery salt, sea salt, and ground white pepper to taste.

FOR THE SALAD:
Yield: 1 serving

1 6-ounce strip steak, fat removed
Pinch of sea salt
Pinch of ground white pepper
Dash of Old Bay seasoning
2 tablespoons extra virgin olive oil
3 leaves Bibb lettuce, washed, outer leaves of head removed and discarded
2 ounces baby spring mix (or any type of mixed greens)

¼ red onion, peeled, fine julienne

5 quartered artichoke hearts

3 cherry tomatoes, halved

¼ yellow bell pepper, cut into triangles

1⅓ tablespoons scallion buttermilk ranch dressing (see earlier recipe)

¼ cup Asiago cheese, grated

PROCEDURE:

1. Season the strip steak with sea salt, ground white pepper, and a dash of Old Bay seasoning.
2. Heat a small sauté pan over high heat for 10-15 seconds, add the olive oil, and sear the steak on each side and cook in pan for 2 minutes on each side for medium rare.
3. Allow steak to rest for at least 10 minutes at room temperature before slicing. Slice steak into about 5 or 6 equal-sized slices.
4. Lay the leaves of Bibb lettuce on the serving plate at 3:00, 6:00, and 9:00.
5. In a mixing bowl, toss together the mixed greens, red onion, artichokes, cherry tomatoes, and bell peppers with the scallion buttermilk ranch dressing.
6. Place dressed salad onto the Bibb leaves in the center of the serving plate and place sliced strip steak on top of salad.
7. Finish salad by sprinkling it with the grated Asiago cheese and spooning more dressing onto salad if desired. Serve immediately.

NUTRITION FACTS PER SERVING (DRESSING ONLY):

Calories: 33

Protein: 2g

Total Fat: 0g

Saturated Fat: 0g

Cholesterol: 2mg

Carbohydrates: 7g

Fiber: 1g

Sugars: 2g

Calcium: 73mg

Iron: 1mg

NUTRITION FACTS PER SERVING (SALAD ONLY):

Calories: 537

Protein: 35g

Total Fat: 40g

Saturated Fat: 10g

Cholesterol: 90mg

Carbohydrates: 8g

Fiber: 2g

Sugars: 4g

Calcium: 325mg

Iron: 4mg

Roasted Turkey Cobb Salad with Cranberry-Orange Dressing

FOR THE CRANBERRY-ORANGE DRESSING

Yield: 6 servings of 3 tablespoons each

½ can (8 ounces) chunky cranberry sauce

3 tablespoons mandarin orange juice from jar of mandarin oranges

18 segments mandarin oranges

1 tablespoon honey

1 tablespoon mayonnaise

Sea salt to taste

Ground white pepper to taste

PROCEDURE:

1. In a blender, puree the cranberry sauce, mandarin orange juice, and mandarin orange segments until smooth.
2. Transfer puree to a clean mixing bowl and whisk in honey and mayonnaise.
3. Season to taste with sea salt and ground white pepper.

FOR THE SALAD:

Yield: 1 serving

1 head romaine lettuce, washed, julienne

2 ounces spinach, washed, stems removed

3 black olives, sliced

3 tablespoons cranberry-orange dressing (see earlier recipe)

½ red heirloom tomato, ¼ cut into 4 small wedges and ¼ small diced

¼ avocado, peeled and cut into 4 equal-sized wedges

4 strips of turkey bacon, cooked, medium dice

5 ounces roasted turkey breast (all-natural lunchmeat is fine), medium dice

3 yellow cherry tomatoes, halved

PROCEDURE:

1. In a mixing bowl, toss the romaine, spinach, and black olives with 1½ tablespoons of the cranberry-orange dressing.
2. On the serving plate, arrange the wedges of tomato and place the dressed greens on the plate as well.
3. Place the avocado, turkey bacon, turkey breast, diced tomatoes, and yellow cherry tomatoes onto the dressed salad and arrange, such as in a Cobb salad.
4. Drizzle the composed salad with an additional 1½ tablespoons of the cranberry-orange dressing and serve.

NUTRITION FACTS PER SERVING (DRESSING ONLY):

Calories: 88
Protein: 0g
Total Fat: 2g
Saturated Fat: 0g
Cholesterol: 1mg
Carbohydrates: 19g
Fiber: 1g
Sugars: 18g
Calcium: 3mg
Iron: 0mg

NUTRITION FACTS PER SERVING (SALAD ONLY):

Calories: 464
Protein: 48g
Total Fat: 20g
Saturated Fat: 5g
Cholesterol: 102mg
Carbohydrates: 29g
Fiber: 19g
Sugars: 9g
Calcium: 299mg
Iron: 10mg

ROASTED TURKEY COBB SALAD WITH CRANBERRY-ORANGE DRESSING

SALADS 69

Blackened Salmon Salad with Lemon-Dill Dressing

FOR THE LEMON-DILL DRESSING:
Yield: 3 servings of 2 tablespoons each

2½ tablespoons mayonnaise

1 tablespoon fat-free sour cream

1 lemon, zest and juice

1 teaspoon 3-grain mustard

1 tablespoon fresh dill, finely chopped

Pinch of celery salt

Sea salt to taste

Ground white pepper to taste

PROCEDURE:
1. In a mixing bowl, whisk together the mayonnaise, sour cream, lemon zest, lemon juice, mustard, chopped dill, and celery salt until thoroughly combined.
2. Season to taste with sea salt and ground white pepper.

FOR THE SALAD:
Yield: 1 Serving

1 5-ounce filet of wild-caught salmon, skinless and boneless

1 tablespoon Paul Prudhomme's Seafood Magic

1½ tablespoons extra virgin olive oil

1 head romaine lettuce, washed, outer leaves removed, cut into bite-sized pieces

¼ head of radicchio, washed and cut into bite-sized pieces

1 ounce cucumber, peeled, cut lengthwise, seeds scraped out, and sliced about ¼ inch thick

¼ red bell pepper, ribs removed, julienne

¼ yellow bell pepper, ribs removed, julienne

2 tablespoons lemon-dill dressing (see earlier recipe)

½ ounce candied walnuts (can be bought candied, or regular walnuts may be substituted)

3 cherry tomatoes, halved

6 mandarin orange segments

½ ounce Gorgonzola cheese, crumbled

PROCEDURE:
1. Rub the top of the salmon filet with Paul Prudhomme's Seafood Magic to coat.
2. Heat a nonstick sauté pan over high heat for 10-15 seconds, add the olive oil, and sear the top and bottom of the salmon filet. Cook in the sauté pan about 2 minutes on each side or to an internal temperature of 130 degrees.
3. Remove from heat and allow to rest at room temperature for at least 5 minutes before serving.
4. In a mixing bowl, combine the romaine, radicchio, cucumber, red bell pepper, and yellow bell pepper and toss with 1 tablespoon of the lemon-dill dressing.
5. Place the dressed salad onto the serving plate and arrange the candied walnuts, cherry tomatoes, and mandarin orange segments on the salad.
6. Sprinkle the salad with the crumbled Gorgonzola cheese and drizzle an additional tablespoon of the lemon dill dressing.
7. Place the salmon filet on top of the salad and serve.

NUTRITION FACTS PER SERVING (DRESSING ONLY):

Calories: 91

Protein: 1g

Total Fat: 9g

Saturated Fat: 1g

Cholesterol: 7mg

Carbohydrates: 2g

Fiber: 0g

Sugars: 0g

Calcium: 20mg

Iron: 0mg

NUTRITION FACTS PER SERVING (SALAD ONLY):

Calories: 575

Protein: 35g

Total Fat: 35g

Saturated Fat: 7g

Cholesterol: 74mg

Carbohydrates: 37g

Fiber: 17g

Sugars: 19g

Calcium: 351mg

Iron: 8mg

BLACKENED SALMON SALAD WITH LEMON-DILL DRESSING

SALADS 73

NUTRITION FACTS PER SERVING:

Calories: 144

Protein: 1g

Total Fat: 9g

Saturated Fat: 1g

Cholesterol: 0mg

Carbohydrates: 15g

Fiber: 4g

Sugars: 10g

Calcium: 36mg

Iron: 1mg

Mango-Jicama Slaw with Pickled Ginger Vinaigrette

Yield: About 6 servings

FOR THE PICKLED GINGER VINAIGRETTE:

2 tablespoons pickled ginger

3 tablespoons white wine vinegar

5 tablespoons extra virgin olive oil

1 tablespoon honey

½ cup water

½ orange, zest and juice

½ lime, zest and juice

1 tablespoon sweet Asian chili sauce

Sea salt to taste

Ground white pepper to taste

PROCEDURE:

1. In a blender, combine all ingredients and blend on high until thoroughly incorporated.
2. Season to taste with sea salt and ground white pepper.

FOR THE MANGO-JICAMA SLAW:

2 cups Jicama, peeled and grated on a box grater

¼ head red cabbage, chiffonade

½ cup snap peas, blanched and shocked

1 mango, peeled, julienne

1 ounce baby arugula

1 recipe pickled ginger vinaigrette (see earlier recipe)

Sea salt to taste

Ground white pepper to taste

PROCEDURE:

1. In a large mixing bowl, combine the jicama, red cabbage, snap peas, mango, and arugula.
2. Dress the mixture with the pickled ginger vinaigrette.
3. Finish with sea salt and ground white pepper to taste.
4. Serve either chilled or at room temperature.

NUTRITION FACTS PER SERVING:

Calories: 366

Protein: 6g

Total Fat: 20g

Saturated Fat: 3g

Cholesterol: 4mg

Carbohydrates: 41g

Fiber: 7g

Sugars: 5g

Calcium: 68mg

Iron: 2mg

Oven-Roasted Summer Potato Salad

Yield: About 6 servings

WHITE BALSAMIC BLACK PEPPER DRESSING:

2 tablespoons white balsamic vinegar

1 tablespoon fresh cracked black pepper

6 tablespoons extra virgin olive oil

Sea salt to taste

PROCEDURE:

1. Combine the white balsamic vinegar, black pepper, and olive oil in a blender to incorporate.
2. Season to taste with sea salt.

FOR THE POTATO SALAD:

6 baby Yukon Gold potatoes

2 shallots, peeled

1 tablespoon extra virgin olive oil

Sea salt to taste

Ground white pepper to taste

4 ounces green beans, ends removed, blanched, and shocked

12 fresh cherries, pitted and halved

1 ounce walnuts, roasted in a 350-degree oven for 10 minutes and cooled

1 ounce Maytag blue cheese, crumbled

1 recipe white balsamic black pepper dressing (see earlier recipe)

PROCEDURE:

1. In a large mixing bowl, toss the potatoes and shallots with the olive oil and season with sea salt and ground white pepper.
2. Roast the potatoes and shallots in a 350-degree oven for about 30 minutes. A fork or paring knife should easily slide in and out of the center of the potatoes, and the shallots should be caramelized.
3. Allow potatoes and shallots to cool completely at room temperature before assembling the salad.
4. While the potatoes and shallots cool, blanch the green beans for one minute in a pot of boiling salted water. Immediately shock the green beans in an ice bath until thoroughly chilled.
5. When thoroughly chilled, remove green beans from ice bath and towel dry.
6. When the potatoes and shallots are at room temperature, cut the potatoes into discs about ¼ inch thick, and roughly chop the shallots.
7. In a large mixing bowl, toss the potatoes, shallots, green beans, cherries, walnuts, blue cheese, and white balsamic black pepper dressing.
8. Season to taste with sea salt and ground white pepper.

NUTRITION FACTS PER SERVING:

Calories: 161

Protein: 8g

Total Fat: 11g

Saturated Fat: 4g

Cholesterol: 25mg

Carbohydrates: 9g

Fiber: 1g

Sugars: 1g

Calcium: 194mg

Iron: 1mg

Creamy Caprese Salad with Basil Ranch Dressing

Yield: About 6 servings

FOR THE BASIL RANCH DRESSING:

⅔ ounce fresh basil

2½ ounces fresh spinach, stems removed, roughly chopped

4 ounces fat-free sour cream

1 tablespoon mayonnaise

1 tablespoon extra virgin olive oil

2 tablespoons ranch dressing mix from packet

Sea salt to taste

Ground white pepper to taste

PROCEDURE:

1. In a blender, combine the basil, spinach, sour cream, mayonnaise, olive oil, and ranch dressing mix until smooth and creamy.
2. Season to taste with sea salt and ground white pepper.

FOR THE SALAD:

¼ cucumber, peeled

8 ounces fresh mozzarella pearls, drained

7 cherry tomatoes, halved

¼ red onion, peeled, fine julienne

1 recipe basil ranch dressing (see earlier recipe)

1 teaspoon fresh cracked black pepper

Sea salt to taste

PROCEDURE:

1. Cut cucumber in half lengthwise. Use a teaspoon to scrape out the seeds, creating a half-moon shape. Proceed to cut the cucumber into ¼-inch-thick slices and reserve.
2. In a mixing bowl, toss the cucumber, mozzarella, cherry tomatoes, and red onion with the basil ranch dressing.
3. Season with 1 teaspoon fresh cracked black pepper and sea salt to taste.

Sandwich:
a). Two or more slices of bread or a split roll having a filling in between.
b). One slice of bread covered with food.

It is hard to think of a better companion to a salad or great bowl of soup than a sandwich. In fact, I would venture to say that one doesn't exist. It is a match made in heaven. Sandwiches are great for their convenience and their place in American tradition. It's technically a meal on the go that you can eat easily, with no fork and knife required.

So many different types of sandwiches exist, but the one I would like to talk about is the slider. The slider is becoming increasingly popular, and I am a huge fan. It is much more convenient than the half-a-sandwich-and-soup deal that is ever-present on any lunch menu. I mean, really, if you make a sandwich at home to only have half, what do you do with the other half? Why not just make a slider and solve this dilemma? Also, sliders are great for parties and picnics. How many times have you wanted to have a burger and a hotdog but just couldn't eat both with the amount of other foods present? If you have a slider instead, the problem is easily solved. That is the reason we have included some very convenient—and delicious—slider recipes for you to try. If you aren't feeling the slider version, feel free to bulk up the recipe and make full versions of the sandwiches instead. We have also included some full-size sandwich recipes as well, to satisfy the traditionalists among you.

So please, use these sandwiches along with the soup and salad recipes in this book. Find the two that you enjoy the most and make a lunch out of it, or just have a sandwich. Either way, please have fun and enjoy these sandwiches!

SECTION V

Sandwiches

Turkey-Apricot Sliders with Fresh Pickles

Yield: 12 servings of 1 slider each

FOR THE PICKLES:

2 small pickling cucumbers, sliced into thin discs

3 cups water

2 ounces white wine vinegar

2 tablespoons dry mustard

1 tablespoon sugar

2 tablespoons kosher salt

Dash of ground white pepper

1 tablespoon sweet Asian chili sauce

PROCEDURE:

1. Place the sliced cucumbers in a small stainless steel bowl and place the bowl over ice.
2. In a saucepan, combine the water, vinegar, dry mustard, sugar, kosher salt, white pepper, and chili sauce.
3. Bring the liquid to a boil over medium-high heat.
4. After liquid has come to a boil, remove from heat and immediately pour over the cucumbers.
5. Stir gently to be sure that all cucumbers are submerged in the liquid.
6. Allow the pickles to cool in the liquid until they reach room temperature.
7. Once the pickles and the liquid have reached room temperature, place in the refrigerator and allow to sit for at least 24 hours before using as pickles. Pickles should be stored in the liquid.

FOR THE APRICOT GLAZE:

2 tablespoons extra virgin olive oil

1 tablespoon sugar

3 fresh apricots with pits removed, roughly chopped

½ white onion, peeled, small dice (about ½ cup diced)

1 tablespoon honey

2 tablespoons sweet Asian chili sauce

Sea salt to taste

Ground white pepper to taste

PROCEDURE:

1. In a saucepan over low heat, combine the olive oil and the sugar. Cook until the sugar is just dissolved.
2. Turn the heat up to medium-high and immediately add the apricots and the onion and cook for about 2 minutes, stirring occasionally.
3. After cooking for 2 minutes, add the honey and the Asian chili sauce and cook for an additional 1 minute.
4. Remove from heat and season to taste with sea salt and ground white pepper.
5. Place half of the apricot mixture in a blender and puree until smooth. Reserve for the glaze.
6. Place the other half of the apricot mixture in a stainless steel mixing bowl and place over ice while stirring to cool. It is very important to make sure that this half of the mixture is cooled completely before continuing.

FOR THE TURKEY-APRICOT SLIDERS:

24 ounces ground turkey
1 recipe apricot glaze (see earlier recipe)
1 large egg
Pinch of sea salt
Pinch of ground white pepper
12 multigrain flatbreads, trimmed to fit sliders
24 fresh pickle slices (see earlier recipe)—the slices should be julienned
12 teaspoons sweet Asian chili sauce

PROCEDURE:

1. In a mixing bowl, thoroughly combine ground turkey, apricot mixture (the half that was not pureed in the blender and is completely cooled), and the egg.
2. Season the turkey mixture with sea salt and ground white pepper.
3. Divide the turkey mixture into 2-ounce portions and form into patties.
4. Grill on high heat for about 5 to 6 minutes per side. The internal temperature of each patty should be 165 degrees.
5. To assemble, place one patty on the bottom of the flatbread, spread a layer of the pureed apricot glaze directly onto turkey patty, place the julienned pickles on top of the glaze, add the Asian chili sauce over the pickles, and finish with the top of the flatbread. Serve immediately.

TURKEY-APRICOT SLIDERS WITH FRESH PICKLES

NUTRITION FACTS PER SERVING:

Calories: 126

Protein: 10g

Total Fat: 7g

Saturated Fat: 2g

Cholesterol: 62mg

Carbohydrates: 4g

Fiber: 0g

Sugars: 4g

Calcium: 12mg

Iron: 1mg

Crab Cake Sliders with Orange-Mustard Aioli

Yield: 8 servings of 1 slider each

FOR THE ORANGE-MUSTARD AIOLI:

2 tablespoons mayonnaise

1 tablespoon whole-grain mustard

1 orange, zest only plus juice from half of the orange

Sea salt to taste

Ground white pepper to taste

PROCEDURE:

1. In a mixing bowl, whisk mayonnaise, whole-grain mustard, orange zest, and orange juice until thoroughly combined.
2. Season to taste with sea salt and ground white pepper.

FOR THE CRAB CAKE SLIDERS:

1 tablespoon extra virgin olive oil

1 green bell pepper, small dice

½ white onion, peeled, small dice

1 stalk of celery, small dice

2 tablespoons Old Bay seasoning

1 16-ounce can crab meat, drained

2 tablespoons mayonnaise

2 tablespoons fat-free sour cream

3 tablespoons liquid egg whites

1 tablespoon grated Parmesan cheese

1 teaspoon sea salt

½ teaspoon ground white pepper

1 cup bread crumbs

2 tablespoons extra virgin olive oil

8 small dinner rolls, trimmed to fit slider

6 inner leaves romaine lettuce, chiffonade

4 ounces fennel, fine julienne

1 recipe orange-mustard aioli (see earlier recipe)

PROCEDURE:
1. Heat a medium-sized sauté pan over medium-high heat for 10–15 seconds, add the olive oil, and sauté the green pepper, onion, and celery for about 3 minutes. Season the vegetables with Old Bay seasoning while sautéing.
2. Remove the vegetables from pan and refrigerate to cool mixture completely.
3. After mixture is completely cooled, thoroughly combine the mixture with the crab meat, mayonnaise, fat-free sour cream, egg whites, Parmesan cheese, sea salt, and white pepper in a mixing bowl.
4. Portion crab cake mixture into 2-ounce portions, dust with bread crumbs, and form into patties.
5. In a sauté pan, heat the olive oil over medium heat until it is hot but not smoking.
6. Sauté the crab cakes on each side until they are golden brown.
7. Place the sautéed crab cakes onto paper towels to remove any excess oil.
8. Lightly grill or toast the trimmed dinner rolls to give them some texture.
9. To assemble, place a crab cake onto the bottom of a grilled/toasted dinner roll, place a small salad of the chiffonaded romaine and julienned fennel directly onto the crab cake, put a small dollop of the orange-mustard aioli on top of the salad, and finish with the top half of the dinner roll. Serve immediately.

NUTRITION FACTS PER SERVING:
Calories: 177
Protein: 15g
Total Fat: 7g
Saturated Fat: 1g
Cholesterol: 55mg
Carbohydrates: 13g
Fiber: 1g
Sugars: 2g
Calcium: 103mg
Iron: 1mg

Cajun Beef Sliders with Creamy Chimichurri

Yield: 6 servings of 1 slider each

FOR THE CREAMY CHIMICHURRI:

½ avocado

1 lime, juice only

1 teaspoon white wine vinegar

1 tablespoon extra virgin olive oil

2 tablespoons red onion, peeled and finely chopped

1 tablespoon celery, finely chopped

½ teaspoon garlic, peeled and chopped

3 tablespoons roasted red pepper, finely chopped (jarred or canned is fine)

Sea salt to taste

Ground white pepper to taste

PROCEDURE:

1. In a mixing bowl, combine avocado, lime juice, white wine vinegar, and olive oil and mix until smooth.
2. Fold the red onion, celery, garlic, and roasted red peppers into the avocado mixture until thoroughly combined.
3. Season to taste with sea salt and ground white pepper.

FOR THE CAJUN BEEF SLIDERS:

6 2–3-ounce portions of beef tenderloin

1 tablespoon extra virgin olive oil

1 tablespoon Paul Prudhomme's Meat Magic

6 tablespoons creamy chimichurri (see earlier recipe)

6 slices Tartuffi or Provolone cheese, trimmed to fit the beef

6 mini ciabatta rolls, split lengthwise and grilled

PROCEDURE:

1. In a mixing bowl, evenly coat the beef with the olive oil and season with Paul Prudhomme's Meat Magic.
2. Grill the seasoned beef for about 3 minutes on high heat and flip.
3. After flipping, spoon about 1 tablespoon of the creamy chimichurri onto the beef.
4. After adding the creamy chimichurri, place a slice of the cheese directly onto the creamy chimichurri.
5. Allow the beef to finish grilling for 2 to 3 minutes and remove from the grill directly to the ciabatta roll.
6. Place the top of the grilled roll onto the slider and serve immediately.

NUTRITION FACTS PER SERVING:

Calories: 239
Protein: 15g
Total Fat: 19g
Saturated Fat: 7g
Cholesterol: 48mg
Carbohydrates: 2g
Fiber: 1g
Sugars: 1g
Calcium: 122mg
Iron: 1mg

CAJUN BEEF SLIDERS WITH CREAMY CHIMICHURRI

SANDWICHES 93

Grilled Vegetable Sandwich with Roasted Shallot Hummus

FOR THE ROASTED SHALLOT HUMMUS:
Yield: About 10 servings of 1 ounce each

3 large roasted shallots
1 tablespoon extra virgin olive oil
1 can garbanzo beans, half of the liquid drained
½ teaspoon sea salt
¼ teaspoon ground white pepper

PROCEDURE:
1. Rub shallots with olive oil and wrap in foil. Roast the shallots in a 250-degree oven for one hour.
2. After shallots are roasted, refrigerate to chill completely before proceeding.
3. Place all ingredients in a food processor and puree until smooth.
4. Transfer hummus to a clean bowl and cover. Refrigerate until ready to use.

FOR THE GRILLED VEGETABLE SANDWICH:
Yield: 1 sandwich

1 yellow squash, sliced ¼ inch thick (3 slices per sandwich)
1 zucchini, sliced ¼ inch thick (3 slices per sandwich)
1 portobello mushroom, stem and gills removed and ends trimmed
1 Roma tomato, sliced lengthwise into 3 slices
1 slice medium-sized red onion, ¼ inch thick
2 tablespoons extra virgin olive oil
1½ tablespoons Paul Prudhomme's Vegetable Magic
2 slices multigrain bread
2 slices jalapeno jack cheese
1 recipe roasted shallot hummus (see earlier recipe)

PROCEDURE:

1. In a large mixing bowl, toss all vegetables with the extra virgin olive oil and Paul Prudhomme's Vegetable Magic.
2. Grill each vegetable (except portobello mushroom) at 350 degrees for approximately 8 minutes on 1 side only. For portobello mushroom, grill at same temperature for 4 minutes and then flip to other side for final 4 minutes (turn once during grilling).
3. Remove vegetables from grill and place aside on a clean plate until ready to assemble sandwich.
4. Place multigrain bread on grill and grill on each side just until grill marks appear.
5. To assemble sandwich:
    - Place one slice of jalapeno jack cheese on each slice of bread
    - Spread a thin layer of the roasted shallot hummus on top of each sandwich half
    - Build the sandwich on one slice of the bread (already layered with the cheese and hummus)
    - Arrange in the following order:
        - Zucchini
        - Red onion
        - Tomato
        - Portobello mushroom
        - Yellow squash
6. Place the other piece of dressed bread on the top to complete the sandwich.
7. Sandwich can be served hot or chilled.

NUTRITION FACTS PER SERVING (HUMMUS ONLY):

Calories: 38
Protein: 1g
Fat: 1g
Saturated Fat: 0g
Cholesterol: 0mg
Carbohydrates: 5g
Fiber: 1g
Sugars: 0g
Calcium: 11mg
Iron: 0mg

NUTRITION FACTS PER SERVING (SANDWICH ONLY):

Calories: 353
Protein: 8g
Fat: 32g
Saturated Fat: 7g
Cholesterol: 12mg
Carbohydrates: 13g
Fiber: 4g
Sugars: 5g
Calcium: 145mg
Iron: 2mg

GRILLED VEGETABLE SANDWICH WITH ROASTED SHALLOT HUMMUS

SANDWICHES 97

Shrimp and Egg Salad Sandwich

Yield: 3 servings of 1 sandwich each

4 large eggs

4 ounces 51/60 count shrimp, peeled and deveined

1 tablespoon extra virgin olive oil

¼ tablespoon Paul Prudhomme's Seafood Magic

1½ tablespoons roasted red pepper, canned, brunoise

1 tablespoon fresh dill, chopped

1 tablespoon mayonnaise

2 tablespoons fat-free sour cream

½ tablespoon brown mustard

1 teaspoon Worcestershire sauce

Celery salt to taste

Sea salt to taste

Ground white pepper to taste

3 dinner rolls, split

9 slices Roma tomato, ⅛ inch thick

Fresh cracked black pepper

3 sprigs fresh dill to garnish

PROCEDURE:

1. Place the eggs in a pot with enough room-temperature water to completely submerge them (water level should be approximately 2 inches above the eggs).
2. Cook the eggs over medium-high heat, being careful to only bring the water to a simmer. Start timing the eggs when the water comes to a simmer and cook for 13 minutes.
3. After 13 minutes, carefully remove the eggs from the water and place under cold running water just until they are cool enough to handle with your hands.
4. Peel the hardboiled eggs and refrigerate to chill completely.
5. Once completely chilled, small dice 2 of the eggs and reserve. Cut the other 2 eggs in half lengthwise, remove the yolks and discard, and reserve the halved whites.
6. In a mixing bowl, toss the shrimp with the olive oil and Paul Prudhomme's Seafood Magic.
7. Heat a small sauté pan over medium-high heat for 10-15 seconds and sauté the shrimp in the dry pan for 3-4 minutes or until they turn pink and are fully cooked.
8. Transfer the cooked shrimp from the pan onto a dinner plate and refrigerate until completely cooled.
9. Proceed to small dice the chilled shrimp and place in a mixing bowl.

10. To the diced shrimp, add the diced hardboiled eggs, red pepper, dill, mayonnaise, sour cream, mustard, and Worcestershire sauce and stir to combine.
11. Season to taste with celery salt, sea salt, and ground white pepper.
12. Spoon about ⅓ of the shrimp salad onto the bottom half of the dinner roll and place on a dinner plate with the top half of the roll to serve.
13. Garnish with the tomato slices seasoned with sea salt and fresh cracked black pepper, and spoon a small amount of the remaining shrimp salad into the halved egg whites. Garnish each egg with a sprig of fresh dill.

NUTRITION FACTS PER SERVING:

Calories: 333

Protein: 19g

Fat: 17g

Saturated Fat: 3g

Cholesterol: 307mg

Carbohydrates: 27g

Fiber: 1g

Sugars: 6g

Calcium: 142mg

Iron: 4mg

SHRIMP AND EGG SALAD SANDWICH

Entrée:
The main course of a meal in the United States.

Well, it is time for the coup de grace, if you will. The entrée is most likely the section of this book that you will use the most. Before further discussion of different entrées, I would like to make it clear that you may most certainly use any of the recipes in this book as an entrée. They can either be lighter entrées, or you may simply bulk up the size a bit to an acceptable entrée-sized portion.

    Also, please feel free to mix and match different vegetable, starch, and sauce combinations with the different proteins prepared in this section. We have paired all dishes in a way that the flavor profiles technically match; however, taste is very subjective. Just because we like the way the dishes are put together doesn't necessarily mean you may not like some other combination better. Try new things and make new discoveries. Changing things up is what makes life interesting.

    Most of the entrees are higher in calories than the other recipes in this book. We have, however, limited each item to between 400 and 600 calories. We also have created these recipes in a way that will maximize flavor and make your dining experience as enjoyable as possible. We have paired some items that may exceed your personal calorie count when eaten together. If this is the case, feel free to look through the other recipes and pair items that are also a bit lower in calories.

    We wanted to give you guided options when it comes to your food choices. We tried to give you a nice balance of variety in all aspects of cooking and eating and allow the final decision of what's for dinner to be up to you. We are very excited for you to try these entrées and really have an enjoyable and exciting meal. Essentially, all the recipes in this book have led up to this point. So please enjoy our entrées, but make the meal your own!

SECTION VI

Entrées

Chili-Glazed Turkey Steaks

Yield: 1 serving

1 tablespoon honey
1 teaspoon extra virgin olive oil
½ teaspoon white balsamic vinegar
1 teaspoon chili powder
¼ teaspoon roasted garlic, finely chopped
4 ounces turkey breast, cut into 2-ounce steaks
Sea salt to taste
Fresh cracked black pepper to taste

PROCEDURE:

1. In a mixing bowl, whisk together the honey, extra virgin olive oil, white balsamic vinegar, chili powder, and garlic.
2. Add the turkey steaks to the bowl with the marinade and coat completely.
3. Cover the bowl and place in the refrigerator for at least 1 hour before proceeding.
4. Grill the turkey on medium-high heat for about 4 minutes on each side or until it reaches an internal temperature of 165 degrees.
5. Season with sea salt and fresh cracked black pepper after removing from grill.
6. Allow turkey steaks to rest at room temperature for at least 10 minutes before serving or cutting.

*You may make additional marinade to brush on the turkey and/or serve as a sauce. Be very careful to not use a sauce that has come in direct contact with raw turkey, as this increases the chances of foodborne illness.

NUTRITION FACTS PER SERVING

Calories: 238
Protein: 28g
Total Fat: 6g
Saturated Fat: 1g
Cholesterol: 69mg
Carbohydrates: 19g
Fiber: 1g
Sugars: 18g
Calcium: 21mg
Iron: 2mg

Sweet Potato Lyonnaise

Yield: 1 serving

4 ounces sweet potatoes (5 slices ¼ inch thick)
1 tablespoon extra virgin olive oil
½ cup red onion, peeled, julienne
¼ medium green bell pepper, julienne
¼ medium red bell pepper, julienne
¼ medium yellow bell pepper, julienne
¼ teaspoon Paul Prudhomme's Vegetable Magic
Sea salt to taste
Fresh cracked black pepper to taste

PROCEDURE:

1. Cut sweet potatoes into ¼-inch slices. Trim slices with a round cutter just big enough to remove the skin.
2. In a mixing bowl, toss sweet potato slices with ¾ tablespoon extra virgin olive oil and grill over medium-high heat for 4 minutes on each side.
3. While potatoes are grilling, in a very hot sauté pan, sauté the red onion, green pepper, red pepper, and yellow pepper in ¼ tablespoon extra virgin olive oil. Season the onions and peppers with Paul Prudhomme's Vegetable Magic while cooking.
4. Place grilled potatoes on a serving plate and top with sautéed peppers and onions. Season with sea salt and fresh cracked black pepper.

NUTRITION FACTS PER SERVING:

Calories: 260
Protein: 3g
Total Fat: 14g
Saturated Fat: 2g
Cholesterol: 0mg
Carbohydrates: 33g
Fiber: 6g
Sugars: 10g
Calcium: 55mg
Iron: 1mg

Grilled Asparagus

Yield: 1 serving

5 small pencil spears of asparagus

1 teaspoon extra virgin olive oil

½ tablespoon fresh lemon juice

½ teaspoon fresh lemon zest

Sea salt to taste

Fresh cracked black pepper to taste

PROCEDURE:

1. In a mixing bowl, toss asparagus with olive oil, lemon juice, lemon zest, sea salt, and fresh cracked black pepper.
2. Grill the asparagus on medium-high heat for 8 minutes, turning occasionally.
3. Grilled asparagus can be served hot or chilled.

NUTRITION FACTS PER SERVING:

Calories: 260

Protein: 3g

Total Fat: 14g

Saturated Fat: 2g

Cholesterol: 0mg

Carbohydrates: 33g

Fiber: 6g

Sugars: 10g

Calcium: 55mg

Iron: 1mg

Horseradish-Crusted Salmon

Yield: 1 serving

2 tablespoons plain breadcrumbs

1 teaspoon horseradish from a jar

Olive oil–flavored nonstick cooking spray

1 5-ounce skinless salmon filet

PROCEDURE:

1. In a mixing bowl, combine the breadcrumbs and the horseradish thoroughly to prepare the horseradish crust.
2. Using the nonstick cooking spray, lightly spray a baking sheet and the top of the salmon filet.
3. Cover the top of the salmon filet generously with the horseradish crust and bake in a 250-degree oven for about 24 minutes or until the internal temperature of the salmon reaches 130 degrees.
4. Allow salmon to rest for at least 5 minutes at room temperature before serving.

*Please use wild-caught seafood in preparing any dish that you will serve or consume. The feed that farm-raised fish and other sea creatures are given can make them very harmful to your health.

NUTRITION FACTS PER SERVING:

Calories: 227

Protein: 29g

Total Fat: 9g

Saturated Fat: 1g

Cholesterol: 77mg

Carbohydrates: 5g

Fiber: 0g

Sugars: 1g

Calcium: 31mg

Iron: 1mg

Papaya Ginger Sauce

Yield: About 4 servings

1 papaya, peeled and roughly chopped
4 teaspoons white wine vinegar
½ teaspoon fresh ginger, peeled and grated
1 teaspoon honey
1 tablespoon water
Sea salt to taste
Ground white pepper to taste

PROCEDURE:

1. In a blender, combine the papaya, white wine vinegar, grated ginger, honey, and water and puree until smooth.
2. If the sauce is a bit thick, simply add more water, a little at a time, blending between additions until the desired thickness is achieved.
3. Season with sea salt and ground white pepper to taste.

*Sauce should be allowed to sit for at least 30 minutes prior to serving. Allowing it to sit will allow the ginger flavor to develop. The sauce can either be served at room temperature or chilled, depending on your personal preference.

NUTRITION FACTS PER SERVING:

Calories: 36
Protein: 0g
Total Fat: 0g
Saturated Fat: 0g
Cholesterol: 0mg
Carbohydrates: 9g
Fiber: 1g
Sugars: 6g
Calcium: 19mg
Iron: 0mg

Red Beet Couscous

Yield: About 6 servings

1 can (8¼ ounces) red beets

5 ounces organic vegetable stock

5 ounces couscous

Sea salt to taste

Ground white pepper to taste

PROCEDURE:

1. In a blender, combine the red beets and the organic vegetable stock and puree until completely smooth.
2. Transfer contents from blender into a small saucepan and bring to a boil.
3. While beet liquid is coming to a boil, place couscous in a soufflé crock or a container with a flat bottom to ensure a level surface area.
4. Season the raw couscous with sea salt and ground white pepper. You can always season it again later, but you want the couscous to absorb some flavor while it is steeping.
5. Once the liquid has come to a boil, pour it over the couscous, stir quickly to ensure that the liquid is dispersed evenly, and immediately cover tightly with plastic wrap.
6. Allow the couscous to sit and steep for about 1 minute and then remove the plastic, stir, taste, season, and serve.

NUTRITION FACTS PER SERVING:

Calories: 94

Protein: 3g

Total Fat: 0g

Saturated Fat: 0g

Cholesterol: 0mg

Carbohydrates: 19g

Fiber: 1g

Sugars: 1g

Calcium: 8mg

Iron: 1mg

Roasted Cauliflower and Sugar Snap Peas

Yield: 1 serving

3 medium-sized florets cauliflower, about 2 ounces total

1 teaspoon extra virgin olive oil

6 sugar snap peas, ends trimmed

¼ cup organic vegetable stock

Sea salt to taste

Ground white pepper to taste

PROCEDURE:

1. In a mixing bowl, toss the cauliflower with the extra virgin olive oil.
2. Cauliflower can either be browned in a sauté pan over medium-high heat or in a 400-degree oven. Either way you choose, watch it closely, because it will burn quickly. The cauliflower should be golden brown and cooked thoroughly but not mushy.
3. Combine the sugar snap peas and the vegetable stock in a sauté pan over medium-high heat and cook for about 30 seconds and remove from stock. You should begin timing when the stock comes to a boil. The sugar snap peas should also be cooked thoroughly and should be bright green and al dente.
4. Season the cauliflower and sugar snap peas with sea salt and ground white pepper and serve.

NUTRITION FACTS PER SERVING:

Calories: 61

Protein: 2g

Total Fat: 5g

Saturated Fat: 1g

Cholesterol: 0mg

Carbohydrates: 4g

Fiber: 2g

Sugars: 2g

Calcium: 21mg

Iron: 1mg

HORSERADISH-CRUSTED SALMON WITH PAPAYA GINGER SAUCE, RED BEET COUSCOUS, AND ROASTED CAULIFLOWER AND SUGAR SNAP PEAS

ENTRÉES 113

Rolled Vegetable Lasagna with Basil-Pesto Cream

FOR THE BASIL-PESTO CREAM:
Yield: 4 servings

½ cup heavy cream

2 teaspoons premade basil pesto, from a jar

Dash of celery salt

Dash of cayenne pepper

1 tablespoon slurry

1 tomato, concasse

> *To concasse a tomato, first remove the core and lightly score the bottom of the tomato in an *X* shape. Drop the tomato in boiling water for 30 seconds and then quickly remove from boiling water and drop into ice water to shock the tomato. When the tomato is completely cooled, peel the skin and discard it. Cut the tomato into quarters and filet out the seeds. Discard the seeds, and small dice the remaining filets of tomato.

PROCEDURE:

1. In a saucepan over medium heat, whisk together the cream, pesto, celery salt, and cayenne pepper.
2. When cream begins to boil, whisk in slurry and return to a boil and remove from heat.
3. Fold in tomato concasse and serve.

FOR THE LASAGNA:
Yield: 4 servings of 1 roll each

2 tablespoons extra virgin olive oil

1 yellow squash, julienne

1 green zucchini, julienne

1 red bell pepper, julienne

12 asparagus tips

1 cup Ricotta cheese

¼ cup Asiago cheese, grated

¼ cup Parmesan cheese, grated

Dash of celery salt

Dash of cayenne pepper

4 whole-wheat lasagna noodles, cooked and chilled

1 recipe basil-pesto cream (see earlier recipe)

PROCEDURE:

1. Heat a medium-sized sauté pan over medium-high heat for 10-15 seconds. Add the olive oil and sauté the squash, zucchini, red bell pepper, and asparagus tips until al dente. This should take about 5 minutes.
2. Transfer the vegetables from the pan onto a dinner plate and refrigerate to completely cool before proceeding.
3. After the vegetables are cooled, fold together the vegetables, Ricotta cheese, Asiago cheese, Parmesan cheese, celery salt, and cayenne in a mixing bowl until thoroughly combined.
4. Portion filling into 4-ounce bundles and wrap each bundle in the cooked and chilled lasagna noodles.
5. Place the rolled lasagna on a sprayed sheet pan and cover with foil. Bake at 350 degrees for 15 minutes. The internal temperature of each roll should be 150 degrees.
6. Place lasagna on dinner plates, spoon basil-pesto cream over each roll, and serve.

NUTRITION FACTS PER SERVING:

Calories: 383

Protein: 16g

Total Fat: 27g

Saturated Fat: 13g

Cholesterol: 83mg

Carbohydrates: 20g

Fiber: 3g

Sugars: 3g

Calcium: 354mg

Iron: 2mg

ROLLED VEGETABLE LASAGNA WITH BASIL-PESTO CREAM

116   THE GOOD, THE BAD, THE COOKBOOK

ENTRÉES 117

Crabmeat-Stuffed Flounder

FOR THE CRABMEAT STUFFING:

Yield: 7 servings

1 16-ounce can jumbo lump crabmeat

2 tablespoons mayonnaise

1 tablespoon fat-free sour cream

1 tablespoon fresh chives, chopped

Sea salt to taste

Ground white pepper to taste

Dash of celery salt

Dash of Old Bay seasoning

¼ cup panko bread crumbs

1 teaspoon Asiago cheese, grated

1 teaspoon Parmesan cheese, grated

PROCEDURE:

1. In a mixing bowl, fold together all ingredients until thoroughly combined.
2. Divide into 7 portions of 2½ ounces each and reserve.

FOR THE FLOUNDER:

Yield: 7 servings

7 4-ounce flounder filets, trimmed to uniform rectangles

Sea salt to taste

Ground white pepper to taste

1 recipe crabmeat stuffing (see earlier recipe), 7 portions of 2½ ounces each

2 tablespoons Old Bay seasoning

2 tablespoons fennel fronds, finely chopped

PROCEDURE:

1. Season each flounder filet with sea salt and ground white pepper.
2. Lay each flounder filet out and roll one portion of crabmeat stuffing in each filet from end to end.
3. Combine the Old Bay seasoning with the finely chopped fennel fronds and sprinkle a light layer onto the outside of each stuffed flounder filet.
4. Place the stuffed flounder onto a sprayed baking sheet and bake in a 250-degree oven for about 45 minutes. The internal temperature of the flounder (not the stuffing) should be 135 degrees.

NUTRITION FACTS PER SERVING:

Calories: 295

Protein: 48g

Total Fat: 9g

Saturated Fat: 2g

Cholesterol: 174mg

Carbohydrates: 0g

Fiber: 0g

Sugars: 0g

Calcium: 170mg

Iron: 2mg

Stewed Tomatoes and Fennel

Yield: About 7 servings

1 tablespoon extra virgin olive oil

1 ounce sweet white onion, peeled, small dice

1½ ounces celery, small dice

4 ounces fennel, julienne

1 teaspoon garlic, peeled and minced

1 can (14.5 ounces) diced tomatoes

1 tablespoon slurry

Sea salt to taste

Ground white pepper to taste

Dash of celery salt

Dash of cayenne pepper

2 ounces organic vegetable stock

PROCEDURE:

1. Heat saucepan over medium-high heat for 10–15 seconds. Add the olive oil and sauté the onion, celery, and fennel for about 4 minutes.
2. After 4 minutes, add the minced garlic and sauté for an additional 1 minute to sweat the garlic.
3. Add the diced tomatoes to the saucepan and reduce the heat to a simmer (medium-low). Allow sauce to simmer for 10 minutes while stirring occasionally.
4. After simmering for 10 minutes, add the slurry to thicken slightly, then remove from heat.
5. Season to taste with sea salt, ground white pepper, celery salt, and cayenne pepper. You may thin the sauce down with 2 ounces of vegetable stock if desired.

NUTRITION FACTS PER SERVING:

Calories: 41

Protein: 1g

Total Fat: 2g

Saturated Fat: 0g

Cholesterol: 0mg

Carbohydrates: 5g

Fiber: 1g

Sugars: 2g

Calcium: 35mg

Iron: 1mg

Basil Smashed Red Skin Potatoes

Yield: 5 servings

8 medium-sized red skin potatoes

1 tablespoon extra virgin olive oil

Dash of sea salt

Dash of fresh cracked black pepper

⅔ ounce fresh basil (1 package), stems removed, chopped

1 teaspoon organic butter, softened

1 tablespoon fat-free sour cream

2 tablespoons extra virgin olive oil

⅓ cup organic vegetable stock

Sea salt to taste

Ground white pepper to taste

Dash of celery salt

PROCEDURE:

1. In a mixing bowl, toss the potatoes with the 1 tablespoon of olive oil to coat, then season with sea salt and cracked black pepper.
2. Place on a sheet pan and roast in a 350-degree oven for about 25 minutes or until fork-tender.
3. Once the potatoes are fork-tender, return to a mixing bowl and smash using a potato masher.
4. Add the chopped basil, softened butter, sour cream, 2 tablespoons of olive oil, and vegetable stock to the potatoes and stir until thoroughly combined.
5. Season to taste with sea salt, ground white pepper, and a dash of celery salt.

NUTRITION FACTS PER SERVING:

Calories: 320

Protein: 6g

Total Fat: 9g

Saturated Fat: 2g

Cholesterol: 2mg

Carbohydrates: 54g

Fiber: 8g

Sugars: 4g

Calcium: 40mg

Iron: 2mg

Iron: 2mg

Medley of Yellow Squash and Green Beans

Yield: 1 serving

1½ ounces green beans, ends snipped
1 teaspoon extra virgin olive oil
1½ ounces yellow squash, julienne
Celery salt to taste
Cayenne pepper to taste

PROCEDURE:

1. Blanch the green beans in boiling water for about 1 minute, until al dente. Immediately shock the beans in ice water upon removing them from the boiling water. Once completely cool, remove from ice water and dab dry with a clean towel.
2. Heat a sauté pan over medium-high heat for 10–15 seconds, add the olive oil, and sauté the blanched green beans and yellow squash for 2–3 minutes, until fully cooked.
3. Season vegetables to taste with celery salt and cayenne pepper.

NUTRITION FACTS PER SERVING:

Calories: 61
Protein: 1g
Total Fat: 5g
Saturated Fat: 1g
Cholesterol: 0mg
Carbohydrates: 5g
Fiber: 2g
Sugars: 1g
Calcium: 24mg
Iron: 1mg

Cashew and Coconut–Crusted Chicken Breast

Yield: 2 servings

FOR THE CASHEW AND COCONUT CRUST:

½ cup cashews, chopped

¼ cup panko bread crumbs

¼ cup coconut flakes

Dash of chili powder

Sea salt to taste

Ground white pepper to taste

PROCEDURE:

1. Prepare crust by combining all ingredients.

FOR THE CHICKEN BREAST:

2 tablespoons all-purpose flour

1 large egg and 1 tablespoon water, beaten together

1 recipe cashew and coconut crust (see earlier recipe)

2 5-ounce chicken breasts, skinless and boneless

1 tablespoon extra virgin olive oil

PROCEDURE:

1. Using small mixing bowls, arrange a breading station in the following order, with each ingredient in an individual bowl: the flour, the egg wash (egg and water beaten together), and then the cashew and coconut crust.
2. Dredge the chicken breasts first in the flour, then dip into the egg wash, and finally bread with the cashew and coconut crust.
3. Heat a sauté pan over medium heat for 10-15 seconds, add the olive oil, and sauté the breaded chicken breasts on both sides until the crust becomes golden brown, about 2-3 minutes on each side.
4. Transfer the browned chicken from the pan to a sprayed baking sheet and bake in a 350-degree oven until the chicken breasts have reached an internal temperature of 165 degrees, about 12–15 minutes.
5. Allow chicken breasts to rest at room temperature for at least 5 minutes before slicing and serving.

Peach and Chili Sauce

Yield: 5 servings

1 peach with pit removed, roughly chopped

2 tablespoons Heinz chili sauce

1⅓ tablespoons honey

1 tablespoon soy sauce

¾ cup organic vegetable stock

1 tablespoon raspberry vinegar

1 teaspoon chili powder

1 tablespoon extra virgin olive oil

1 tablespoon coconut flakes

Sea salt to taste

Ground white pepper to taste

PROCEDURE:

1. In a saucepan over medium heat, combine the chopped peach, chili sauce, honey, soy sauce, vegetable stock, raspberry vinegar, and chili powder and bring to a boil.
2. When sauce reaches a boil, immediately reduce to a simmer. Simmer for 7–10 minutes or just until the peach is fork-tender.
3. Transfer sauce to a blender and puree until smooth.
4. When sauce becomes smooth, blend on low speed while slowly drizzling in the olive oil.
5. Add the coconut flakes and slowly pulse in the blender until just incorporated.
6. Season to taste with sea salt and ground white pepper.

Stir-Fry Vegetables

Yield: 2 servings

1 tablespoon extra virgin olive oil

2 ounces cauliflower, cut into small florets

2 ounces broccoli, cut into small florets

2 ounces carrots, peeled, sliced thin on a bias

2 ounces yellow squash, small dice

2 ounces red bell peppers, cut into medium triangles

1 tablespoon soy sauce

1 teaspoon Sriracha chili sauce

Sea salt to taste

Ground white pepper to taste

PROCEDURE:

1. In a very hot sauté pan over high heat, add the olive oil and sauté the vegetables for 3–5 minutes. The vegetables should be cut small enough that they cook quickly to al dente.
2. After 3–5 minutes of cooking, add the soy sauce and Sriracha to the pan and sauté an additional 2 minutes.
3. Season to taste with sea salt and ground white pepper.

NUTRITION FACTS PER SERVING:

Calories: 109

Protein: 3g

Total Fat: 7g

Saturated Fat: 1g

Cholesterol: 0mg

Carbohydrates: 10g

Fiber: 3g

Sugars: 4g

Calcium: 39mg

Iron: 1mg

NUTRITION FACTS PER SERVING (FOR THE CHICKEN ONLY):

Calories: 436

Protein: 36g

Total Fat: 25g

Saturated Fat: 11g

Cholesterol: 171mg

Carbohydrates: 18g

Fiber: 3g

Sugars: 3g

Calcium: 41mg

Iron: 4mg

NUTRITION FACTS PER SERVING (FOR THE PEACH AND CHILI SAUCE ONLY)

Calories: 78

Protein: 1g

Total Fat: 5g

Saturated Fat: 2g

Cholesterol: 0mg

Carbohydrates: 9g

Fiber: 1g

Sugars: 7g

Calcium: 6mg

Iron: 0mg

CASHEW AND COCONUT–CRUSTED CHICKEN BREAST WITH PEACH AND CHILI SAUCE AND STIR-FRY VEGETABLES

Bacon-Wrapped Mesquite-Marinated Pork Loin

Yield: 5 servings

12 1-ounce strips of uncured bacon

Dash of ground white pepper

Dash of chili powder

1 mesquite-marinated pork loin, can be bought already marinated, fat trimmed

PROCEDURE:

1. Lay out strips of bacon so that they are all touching and form one sheet. Apply light pressure to the bacon to help the strips hold together.
2. Season the bacon with the ground white pepper and chili powder.
3. Roll the marinated pork loin completely in the bacon, from top to bottom, until it is wrapped all the way around.
4. Place the wrapped pork loin on a sprayed baking sheet and roast in a 400-degree oven for 30 minutes.
5. After 30 minutes, turn the oven temperature up to 450 degrees and roast for an additional 15 minutes. Total roasting time should be about 45 minutes, and the internal temperature of the cooked pork loin should be 165 degrees.
6. Allow roasted pork loin to rest at room temperature for at least 10 minutes before slicing into 2½-ounce slices. Each person should receive 2 slices of 2½ ounces each.

NUTRITION FACTS PER SERVING:

Calories: 469

Protein: 36g

Total Fat: 35g

Saturated Fat: 12g

Cholesterol: 133mg

Carbohydrates: 0g

Fiber: 0g

Sugars: 0g

Calcium: 11mg

Iron: 2mg

Dried Cranberry Sauce

Yield: 5 servings

1 cup water
2 tablespoons red wine vinegar
½ cup dried cranberries
1 teaspoon chili powder
¼ cup honey
1 tablespoon slurry
1 orange, zest only
Sea salt to taste
Ground white pepper to taste

PROCEDURE:
1. In a saucepan over medium-high heat, combine the water, red wine vinegar, dried cranberries, chili powder, and honey and simmer for about 10 minutes.
2. After simmering for 10 minutes, add the 1 tablespoon of slurry and bring to a boil.
3. When sauce comes to a boil, remove from heat and add the orange zest.
4. Season to taste with sea salt and ground white pepper.

NUTRITION FACTS PER SERVING:

Calories: 92
Protein: 0g
Total Fat: 0g
Saturated Fat: 0g
Cholesterol: 0mg
Carbohydrates: 24g
Fiber: 1g
Sugars: 22g
Calcium: 5mg
Iron: 0mg

Sweet Corn and Red Pepper Risotto

Yield: 6 servings

2 tablespoons extra virgin olive oil

2 teaspoons organic butter

2 ounces white onion, peeled, small dice

3 ounces red bell pepper, small dice

3 ounces corn, canned, drained

1 cup arborio rice

2½ cups organic vegetable stock, simmering

⅔ cup heavy cream

2 tablespoons Parmesan cheese, grated

Sea salt to taste

Ground white pepper to taste

PROCEDURE:

1. Heat a saucepan over medium-high heat for 10–15 seconds; add the olive oil and butter; and sweat the onion, red bell pepper, and corn for about 2–3 minutes.
2. Add the arborio rice to the pan and sauté, while stirring constantly with a wooden spoon or rubber spatula, until it begins to give off a nutty aroma. Be careful not to burn the rice.
3. As soon as it begins to smell nutty, add about 7 ounces of the simmering vegetable stock to the rice, while still stirring continuously.
4. As soon as the rice absorbs the 7 ounces of stock, add an additional 7 ounces and continue to stir. Repeat this step until the rice has absorbed all of the stock. You should add stock to the rice in 3 installments overall, and the average cooking time of arborio rice is about 20 minutes. The rice should be thick, creamy, and fully cooked.
5. Finish the risotto by folding in the cream and grated Parmesan cheese. Season to taste with sea salt and ground white pepper.

NUTRITION FACTS PER SERVING

Calories: 382	Protein: 5g
Total Fat: 26g	Saturated Fat: 14g
Cholesterol: 78mg	Carbohydrates: 32g
Fiber: 2g	Sugars: 1g
Calcium: 63mg	Iron: 2mg

Pan-Roasted Butternut Squash and Brussels Sprouts

Yield: 2 servings

2 teaspoons extra virgin olive oil

1 teaspoon organic butter

3 ounces butternut squash, large dice

3 ounces brussels sprouts, outer leaves removed, cut in half

Sea salt to taste

Ground white pepper to taste

PROCEDURE:

1. Heat a small sauté pan over medium-high heat for 10–15 seconds, add the olive oil and butter, and sauté the butternut squash and brussels sprouts until they caramelize or turn golden brown and are fork-tender, about 5–6 minutes.
2. Season to taste with sea salt and ground white pepper.

NUTRITION FACTS PER SERVING:

Calories: 93

Protein: 2g

Total Fat: 7g

Saturated Fat: 2g

Cholesterol: 5mg

Carbohydrates: 8g

Fiber: 2g

Sugars: 1g

Calcium: 32mg

Iron: 1mg

BACON-WRAPPED MESQUITE-MARINATED PORK LOIN WITH DRIED CRANBERRY SAUCE, SWEET CORN AND RED PEPPER RISOTTO, AND PAN-ROASTED BUTTERNUT SQUASH, AND BRUSSELS SPROUTS

Porcini-Dusted Filet Mignon of Beef

Yield: 6 servings

FOR THE PORCINI DUST:

1 ounce dried porcini mushrooms

1 tablespoon sea salt

Pinch of ground white pepper

PROCEDURE:

1. In a microwave-safe bowl, microwave the dried porcini mushrooms uncovered on high for 30 seconds.
2. Remove the bowl from the microwave and allow the mushrooms to sit for 2–3 minutes at room temperature.
3. After they have sat at room temperature for 2–3 minutes, microwave the mushrooms again on high for an additional 20 seconds, remove the bowl from the microwave, and allow the mushrooms to cool at room temperature for 5 minutes.
4. After cooling, place the mushrooms in a food processor and pulse into a dust.
5. Add the sea salt and white pepper to the porcini dust and reserve.

FOR THE BEEF:

6 5-ounce filets of beef

1 recipe porcini mushroom dust (see earlier recipe)

2 tablespoons extra virgin olive oil

PROCEDURE:

1. Roll each filet in the porcini mushroom dust until it is coated completely.
2. Heat a sauté pan over medium-high heat for 10–15 seconds, add the olive oil, and sear the filets on all sides, just until the porcini dust turns dark. Do not oversear; the dust should darken but not turn dark black and smell burnt.
3. Transfer the seared filets to a sprayed baking sheet and roast in a 250-degree oven to desired doneness. Please refer to the temperature chart in the front of the book.
4. Allow filets to rest for at least 5–7 minutes at room temperature before cutting into them.

Steak Sauce

Yield: 5–6 servings

1 teaspoon extra virgin olive oil

2 ounces white onion, peeled and roughly chopped

½ teaspoon garlic, peeled and minced

¼ cup light brown sugar

¼ cup Worcestershire sauce

1 tablespoon soy sauce

1 tablespoon ketchup

1 tablespoon Heinz chili sauce

¼ cup organic beef stock

1 teaspoon slurry

PROCEDURE:

1. Heat a saucepan over medium-high heat for 10–15 seconds, add the olive oil, and sweat the onions and garlic just until they turn translucent.
2. Once the onions and garlic turn translucent, add the brown sugar to the pan and allow it to melt while stirring constantly.
3. After the brown sugar melts, add the Worcestershire sauce, soy sauce, ketchup, chili sauce, and beef stock and reduce by half.
4. Transfer sauce to a blender and puree until smooth.
5. Return the sauce to the pan and bring it to a boil, add the slurry to slightly thicken, and remove from heat.

NUTRITION FACTS PER SERVING (FOR THE FILET MIGNON ONLY):

Calories: 378

Protein: 27g

Total Fat: 29g

Saturated Fat: 11g

Cholesterol: 95mg

Carbohydrates: 0g

Fiber: 0g

Sugars: 0g

Calcium: 35mg

Iron: 2mg

NUTRITION FACTS PER SERVING (FOR THE STEAK SAUCE ONLY):

Calories: 50

Protein: 1g

Total Fat: 1g

Saturated Fat: 0g

Cholesterol: 0mg

Carbohydrates: 11g

Fiber: 0g

Sugars: 8g

Calcium: 22mg

Iron: 1mg

Cauliflower Puree

Yield: 2 servings

6 ounces cauliflower, cut into florets
½ cup organic vegetable stock
½ cup heavy cream
Sea salt to taste
Ground white pepper to taste

PROCEDURE:

1. In a saucepan over medium-high heat, combine the cauliflower, vegetable stock, and heavy cream and simmer until the cauliflower is fork-tender.
2. Once the cauliflower is fork-tender, transfer the contents of the pan to a blender and puree until smooth.
3. Season to taste with sea salt and ground white pepper.

NUTRITION FACTS PER SERVING:

Calories: 214
Protein: 3g
Total Fat: 21g
Saturated Fat: 13g
Cholesterol: 77mg
Carbohydrates: 6g
Fiber: 2g
Sugars: 2g
Calcium: 55mg
Iron: 0mg

Wilted Arugula with Sun-dried Tomatoes

Yield: 2 servings

1 tablespoon white balsamic vinegar

2 tablespoons extra virgin olive oil

3 sun-dried tomatoes, fine julienne

1 ounce baby arugula, stems removed

Sea salt to taste

Ground white pepper to taste

PROCEDURE:

1. In a saucepan over medium heat, combine the vinegar and olive oil and bring to a simmer. Remove from heat.
2. In a mixing bowl, combine the sun-dried tomatoes and arugula and toss together.
3. Pour the warm vinaigrette over the sun-dried tomatoes and arugula and toss to coat evenly.
4. Season to taste with sea salt and ground white pepper. Serve immediately.

NUTRITION FACTS PER SERVING:

Calories: 160

Protein: 2g

Total Fat: 14g

Saturated Fat: 2g

Cholesterol: 0mg

Carbohydrates: 8g

Fiber: 2g

Sugars: 6g

Calcium: 38mg

Iron: 2mg

PORCINI-DUSTED FILET MIGNON OF BEEF WITH STEAK SAUCE, CAULIFLOWER PUREE, AND WILTED ARUGULA WITH SUN-DRIED TOMATOES

Whole-Wheat Gnocchi with Portobello Mushroom Cream and Tarragon Croissant

FOR THE PORTOBELLO MUSHROOM CREAM
Yield: 8 servings

½ tablespoon extra virgin olive oil
1 package (½ ounce) dried portobello mushrooms
1 tablespoon fresh tarragon leaves
1 teaspoon garlic, peeled and minced
1 cup organic vegetable stock
1 pint heavy cream
1 teaspoon sea salt
½ teaspoon celery salt
Pinch of cayenne pepper
2 tablespoons slurry

PROCEDURE:
1. Heat a saucepan over medium-high heat for 10-15 seconds, add the olive oil, and sauté the dried mushrooms and tarragon for about 2 minutes.
2. After 2 minutes, add the minced garlic to the pan and sauté for an additional 2 minutes.
3. After sweating the garlic, add the vegetable stock to the pan and bring to a boil.
4. Transfer sauce to a blender and puree on low speed until smooth.
5. Return the sauce to the pan and whisk in the heavy cream, sea salt, celery salt, and cayenne pepper.
6. Bring the sauce to a boil, add the slurry to thicken, remove from heat, and reserve.

FOR THE TARRAGON CROISSANTS:

Yield: 8 croissants

1 package premade croissant dough
1 tablespoon fresh tarragon, finely chopped
Sea salt to taste
Fresh cracked black pepper to taste
1 tablespoon Asiago cheese, grated

PROCEDURE:

1. Lay croissant dough out flat on a cutting board.
2. Sprinkle the chopped tarragon onto the croissant dough and, using your hands, lightly press it into the dough.
3. Season the dough with sea salt and cracked black pepper.
4. Sprinkle the dough with the grated Asiago cheese and lightly press again to work some of the cheese into the dough.
5. Flip the dough over so that the seasoned side is now facing down.
6. Roll each croissant into the proper croissant shape as instructed on the package.
7. Place croissants on a sprayed baking sheet and bake at 350 degrees for 11–13 minutes or however long the directions on the package specify.

FOR THE GNOCCHI:

Yield: 4 servings

1 16-ounce package dried whole-wheat gnocchi

1 tablespoon extra virgin olive oil

1 teaspoon organic butter

2 ounces red bell pepper, ribs removed, cut into medium-sized flags

20 asparagus tips

2 portobello mushrooms, gills removed and thickly sliced (5–6 slices per mushroom)

6 ounces jumbo lump crabmeat, canned

20 quartered artichoke hearts from a can or jar

½ recipe portobello mushroom cream (see earlier recipe)

1 tablespoon sea salt

Pinch of fresh cracked black pepper

½ recipe tarragon croissants (see earlier recipe)

PROCEDURE:

1. Bring a pot of water to a boil and add the gnocchi just as the water begins to boil. When gnocchi begin to float, remove them from the water with a slotted spoon.
2. Immediately shock gnocchi in ice water until they are completely chilled, remove from ice water, and dab dry with a clean hand towel.
3. Heat a large sauté pan over high heat for 10-15 seconds; add the olive oil and butter; and sauté the red peppers, asparagus, and mushrooms for about 3 minutes.
4. After about 3 minutes, add the gnocchi and crabmeat to the pan and stir gently with a rubber spatula, being careful to not let the gnocchi stick to the pan.
5. Once the gnocchi begin to heat up, they will begin to stick to the pan. When they just begin to stick, add the artichoke hearts and cook for an additional 2 minutes.
6. After cooking for 2 minutes, add ½ recipe of the portobello mushroom cream to the pan and fold in until incorporated thoroughly and hot throughout.
7. Season with sea salt and fresh cracked black pepper.
8. Serve with the tarragon croissants.

NUTRITION FACTS PER SERVING (FOR THE MUSHROOM CREAM):

Calories: 221

Protein: 1g

Total Fat: 23g

Saturated Fat: 14g

Cholesterol: 82mg

Carbohydrates: 3g

Fiber: 0g

Sugars: 0g

Calcium: 40mg

Iron: 0mg

NUTRITION FACTS PER SERVING (FOR TARRAGON CROISSANTS ONLY):

Calories: 174

Protein: 4g

Total Fat: 9g

Saturated Fat: 5g

Cholesterol: 29mg

Carbohydrates: 19g

Fiber: 1g

Sugars: 5g

Calcium: 24mg

Iron: 1mg

NUTRITION FACTS PER SERVING (EXCLUDING SAUCE AND CROISSANT):

Calories: 98

Protein: 10g

Total Fat: 5g

Saturated Fat: 1g

Cholesterol: 40mg

Carbohydrates: 4g

Fiber: 1g

Sugars: 2g

Calcium: 52mg

Iron: 1mg

WHOLE-WHEAT GNOCCHI WITH PORTOBELLO MUSHROOM CREAM AND TARRAGON CROISSANT

148 THE GOOD, THE BAD, THE COOKBOOK

Creole Chicken Chili with Whole-Grain Cheddar Croutons

FOR THE WHOLE-GRAIN CHEDDAR CROUTONS:

Yield: 5 servings

4 ounces whole-grain bread, large dice

Pinch of sea salt

Pinch of ground white pepper

½ teaspoon chili powder

½ teaspoon ground cumin

½ teaspoon celery salt

1 ounce scallion (green part only), chopped fine

1 teaspoon organic butter, softened

1 tablespoon extra virgin olive oil

1 ounce sharp cheddar cheese, grated on large side of a box grater

PROCEDURE:

1. In a mixing bowl, fold together all ingredients until thoroughly combined.
2. Transfer croutons to a sprayed sheet pan and bake in a 350-degree oven for 30 minutes. Stir halfway through baking to ensure even cooking.

NUTRITION FACTS PER SERVING:

Calories: 56

Protein: 2g

Total Fat: 5g

Saturated Fat: 2g

Cholesterol: 8mg

Carbohydrates: 1g

Fiber: 0g

Sugars: 0g

Calcium: 47mg

Iron: 0mg

FOR THE CHILI:
Yield: 5 servings

1 pound ground chicken

½ pound ground pork

2 ounces white onion, peeled, medium dice

2 ounces red onion, peeled, medium dice

2 ounces celery, medium dice

2 ounces green bell pepper, ribs removed, medium dice

2 ounces red bell pepper, ribs removed, medium dice

2 ounces banana pepper, medium dice

1 tablespoon extra virgin olive oil

1 tablespoon Paul Prudhomme's Poultry Magic

8 ounces smoked turkey sausage, split lengthwise and then sliced

1 heaping tablespoon tomato paste

1 can (14.5 ounces) diced tomatoes

4 ounces black beans, canned

4 ounces kidney beans, canned

2 cups organic chicken stock

1 tablespoon chili powder

1 teaspoon ground cumin

½ teaspoon celery salt

½ teaspoon cayenne pepper

1 teaspoon sea salt

½ teaspoon ground white pepper

¼ cup cornmeal

PROCEDURE:
1. In a Crock-Pot on high setting, add the ground chicken and ground pork.
2. In a mixing bowl, toss the white onion, red onion, celery, green bell pepper, red bell pepper, and banana pepper with the olive oil and Paul Prudhomme's Poultry Magic.
3. Heat a sauté pan over high heat for 10–15 seconds and sauté the vegetables and turkey sausage in the dry pan for about 5 minutes.
4. After 5 minutes, add the tomato paste to the pan and cook about 3 additional minutes (until tomato paste begins to lightly brown).
5. Transfer the contents of the pan to the Crock-Pot with the ground chicken and ground pork.

6. Add the diced tomatoes to the sauté pan that the vegetables were sautéed in and bring to a simmer to deglaze the pan.
7. After reaching a simmer, transfer the diced tomatoes to the Crock-Pot.
8. Add the black beans, kidney beans, chicken stock, chili powder, ground cumin, celery salt, cayenne pepper, sea salt, and ground white pepper to the Crock-Pot, stir, and cook for 1 hour on high setting.
9. After 1 hour, add the cornmeal, stir, and cook an additional 30 minutes. Turn Crock-Pot down to warm setting and serve with the whole-grain cheddar croutons.

NUTRITION FACTS PER SERVING:

Calories: 524

Protein: 37g

Total Fat: 32g

Saturated Fat: 9g

Cholesterol: 146mg

Carbohydrates: 22g

Fiber: 4g

Sugars: 5g

Calcium: 62mg

Iron: 4mg

Vegetable Roulade with Sun-Dried Tomato Cream

FOR THE SUN-DRIED TOMATO CREAM:

Yield: 5 servings

½ cup organic vegetable stock

8 sun-dried tomatoes

½ cup heavy cream

1 tablespoon slurry

Sea salt to taste

Ground white pepper to taste

PROCEDURE:

1. In a small saucepan over medium-high heat, bring the vegetable stock to a simmer, add the sun-dried tomatoes, and remove from heat.
2. Allow the sun-dried tomatoes to sit in the vegetable stock for 30 minutes to reconstitute.
3. In a blender, puree the vegetable stock and reconstituted sun-dried tomatoes.
4. Transfer the sun-dried tomato puree from the blender back into the saucepan, whisk heavy cream into puree, and bring to a simmer.
5. When the sun-dried tomato cream comes to a simmer, whisk in the slurry to thicken, remove from heat, and season to taste with sea salt and ground white pepper.

NUTRITION FACTS PER SERVING:

Calories: 126

Protein: 3g

Total Fat: 9g

Saturated Fat: 6g

Cholesterol: 33mg

Carbohydrates: 10g

Fiber: 2g

Sugars: 6g

Calcium: 34mg

Iron: 2mg

FOR THE VEGETABLE ROULADE:

Yield: 5 servings

3 tablespoons extra virgin olive oil

3 ounces red onion, peeled, small dice

2 ounces banana peppers, small dice

8 ounces green zucchini, just outer part of zucchini, small dice (1 medium zucchini)

8 ounces yellow squash, just outer part of squash, small dice (1 medium squash)

5 ounces crimini mushrooms, stems removed, small dice

2 ounces black olives, sliced

1 tablespoon garlic, peeled and minced

1 cup tomato puree

1 teaspoon celery salt

2 teaspoons sea salt

1 teaspoon ground white pepper

1 package premade pizza dough

⅔ ounce fresh basil, stems removed, chopped

3 tablespoons fresh parsley, stems removed, chopped

6 ounces buffalo mozzarella, small dice, towel dried

3 tablespoons Parmesan cheese, grated

PROCEDURE:

1. Heat a sauté pan over high heat for 10-15 seconds; add the olive oil; and sauté the red onion, banana peppers, zucchini, squash, mushrooms, and black olives for about 5 minutes or until vegetables are fully cooked.
2. After vegetables are cooked, add the garlic, tomato puree, celery salt, sea salt, and ground white pepper to the pan and sauté an additional 2 minutes while stirring constantly.
3. Transfer the vegetables onto a large dinner plate and refrigerate to chill completely before proceeding.
4. After the vegetables are completely chilled, lay the pizza dough flat on a cutting board.
5. Sprinkle the dough with the chopped basil and parsley.
6. Sprinkle the buffalo mozzarella and grated Parmesan cheese onto the herbed pizza dough.
7. Using a clean rubber spatula, spread a layer of the chilled vegetable mixture over the layer of cheese.
8. Roll the dough from top to bottom, like when rolling a jellyroll or nut roll. Be sure to keep all filling inside of roll and leave the ends a bit open to allow steam to escape while baking.
9. Transfer roulade to a sprayed baking sheet and bake in a 375-degree oven for about 40 minutes or until golden brown.

10. Remove from oven and allow roulade to rest at room temperature for 5–10 minutes before cutting.
11. Cut into 4-ounce portions and serve 2 portions per serving.

NUTRITION FACTS PER SERVING:

Calories: 438

Protein: 14g

Total Fat: 30g

Saturated Fat: 9g

Cholesterol: 30mg

Carbohydrates: 30g

Fiber: 5g

Sugars: 5g

Calcium: 268mg

Iron: 3mg

THE
BAD

Throughout this book we have given you some ideas for simple, healthy foods that taste great. Now it's our turn to cut loose and make our point that sometimes it is ok to eat fantastic tasting food that is not necessarily the healthiest of choices. This section is not titled "The Bad" because it is bad food or really that bad for you. It is titled "The Bad" because when we designed these recipes, we focused solely on taste. As professional chefs, we got to just have fun with food and make it taste great. Progress, not perfection, is the key, so in this section we are giving you some of our favorite recipes, regardless of nutrition facts. This is the food that we typically serve at parties or special events where we just want flat-out good eating with no worries of, "Is this good for me?"

It can also be fun to cook and eat this way on occasion to reward yourself for making the commitment to get healthier or lose the extra pounds. By no means am I saying that we—or anyone, for that matter—should eat like this all the time. These recipes are great for special occasions, such as tailgating or birthday parties, or you can also make them for dinner one night per week if you like. Studies show that most people who are on diets fail because they deprive themselves of food they love for so long that it is just a matter of time before they relapse to their old habits. Well, it's a good thing we don't do diets, and we don't deprive ourselves. This entire book is about making a lifestyle change to positively impact your health. We want that change to last and to be as easy as possible. Please enjoy these recipes on occasion, and we know whomever you share them with will enjoy them too.

*Nutrition Facts are not included with the recipes in this chapter. Since you will be indulging with these recipes, go ahead and enjoy it! Ignorance is bliss when you allow yourself to have fun occasionally.

SECTION VII

The Bad

160 THE GOOD, THE BAD, THE COOKBOOK

Deep-Fried Turkey Saltimbocca with Basil Pesto Dipping Sauce

Yield: 5 servings

FOR THE BASIL PESTO DIPPING SAUCE:
2 teaspoons mayonnaise
1 teaspoon basil pesto, from a jar

PROCEDURE:
1. In a mixing bowl, whisk together the mayonnaise and basil pesto until thoroughly incorporated.

FOR THE TURKEY SALTIMBOCCA:
5 slices of raw turkey breast, ¼ inch thick and 2 inches long
Pinch of ground white pepper
1¼ ounces Pecorino cheese, sliced into 5 pieces of ¼ ounce each, the same size as the turkey
5 fresh sage leaves
5 slices prosciutto, sliced as thin as possible
½ cup all-purpose flour
1 large egg and 1 tablespoon water, beaten together
1 cup Ruffles potato chips, crushed into crumbs
Deep-fryer filled with either canola or peanut oil
1 recipe basil pesto dipping sauce (see earlier recipe)
Roasted red pepper, from a can or jar, small dice

PROCEDURE:
1. Lay the slices of turkey breast onto a cutting board and season each piece with a pinch of ground white pepper.
2. Place a slice of the Pecorino cheese on each slice of turkey so they are directly on top of one another, facing the same direction.
3. Place 1 sage leaf on top of each slice of Pecorino cheese.
4. Place each piece of turkey on one end of each piece of prosciutto and roll end to end, completely encasing turkey.
5. In small mixing bowls, prepare a breading station in the following order, with each ingredient in an individual bowl: the flour, egg wash (egg + water beaten together), and the Ruffles potato chip crumbs.
6. Dredge each wrapped piece of turkey first in the flour, then dip in the egg wash, and finally coat in the Ruffles potato chip crumbs.
7. Deep-fry each breaded piece of turkey saltimbocca in canola or peanut oil at 350 degrees for 4–5 minutes until golden brown and the internal temperature of the turkey reaches 165 degrees.
8. Serve warm with a dollop of the basil pesto dipping sauce and a small dice of roasted red pepper.

Peanut Butter and Jelly Grape Balls

Yield: 4 servings

4 ounces cream cheese

1 tablespoon creamy peanut butter

½ tablespoon blackberry jelly

12 red grapes (round-shaped grapes work best)

1 cup graham crackers, crushed into crumbs

PROCEDURE:

1. In a mixing bowl, fold together the cream cheese, peanut butter, and jelly until thoroughly combined. Wrap with plastic wrap and refrigerate for at least 30 minutes before use.
2. After cream cheese mixture is completely chilled, use hands and work as quickly as possible to wrap a layer of the cream cheese mixture around each grape. Roll each grape in your hands once it is coated to form a smooth round shape. The warmer the cream cheese mixture gets, the more difficult it is to work with.
3. When all grapes are rolled in the cream cheese mixture, roll each grape in the graham cracker crumbs to coat, and serve.

*Grapes may be rolled in cream cheese mixture and stored in the refrigerator up to 2 days ahead of time. Do not roll in graham cracker crumbs until right before serving.

Roasted Shallot and Blue Cheese Dip

Yield: 10 servings

8 ounces shallots
2 tablespoons extra virgin olive oil
½ cup mayonnaise
½ cup sour cream
5 ounces blue cheese, crumbled
1 packet ranch seasoning mix
1 teaspoon fresh cracked black pepper
Pinch of cayenne

PROCEDURE:

1. In a baking pan, coat the shallots with the olive oil, cover with foil, and place in a 300-degree oven. Roast shallots for 1 hour and then remove the foil and roast uncovered for an additional 30 minutes. The shallots should be starting to turn golden brown and should be fork-tender.
2. When the shallots are fork-tender, transfer to a dinner plate and refrigerate until completely chilled before proceeding.
3. When shallots are completely chilled, pulse in a clean food processor, or use a knife to chop very fine.
4. In a mixing bowl, fold together the chopped shallots, mayonnaise, sour cream, crumbled blue cheese, ranch seasoning, cracked black pepper, and pinch of cayenne pepper until thoroughly combined.
5. Refrigerate dip for at least 30 minutes prior to serving.

Spicy Langoustine Cheese Ball

Yield: 10 servings

¼ cup mayonnaise

¼ cup sour cream

8 ounces cream cheese

2 ounces Asiago cheese, grated

1 teaspoon lemon zest

½ teaspoon sea salt

Pinch of ground white pepper

1 ounce red bell pepper, ribs removed, small dice

1 ounce celery, small dice

1 ounce white onion, peeled, small dice

2 ounces canned corn, drained

6 ounces langoustines, purchased frozen and thawed for use

2 tablespoons extra virgin olive oil

1 tablespoon Old Bay seasoning

1 tablespoon fresh tarragon leaves, chopped

¼ cup Heinz chili sauce

PROCEDURE:

1. In a mixing bowl, fold together the mayonnaise, sour cream, cream cheese, grated Asiago cheese, lemon zest, sea salt, and white pepper until thoroughly combined. Refrigerate to allow the cheese ball to begin to set up.
2. In a different mixing bowl, toss the red bell pepper, celery, onion, corn, and langoustines with 2 tablespoons of olive oil, Old Bay seasoning, and chopped tarragon until thoroughly combined.
3. Heat a sauté pan over medium-high heat for 10–15 seconds; add the langoustines and seasoned vegetables and sauté for about 3 minutes.
4. Transfer the mixture onto a clean dinner plate and refrigerate to chill completely before proceeding.
5. When the mixture is chilled, fold it into the chilled cream cheese mixture until thoroughly combined.
6. Place the cheese ball on a sheet of plastic wrap and wrap into a ball shape and refrigerate for at least 30 minutes before serving.
7. To serve, remove from plastic wrap, making sure to keep the ball shape, and pour the Heinz chili sauce over the top of the cheese ball. Serve with a variety of crackers.

Spicy Sausage and 5-Cheese Dip

Yield: 15 servings

1 pound bulk hot sausage

4 ounces green bell pepper, ribs removed, small dice

4 ounces red bell pepper, ribs removed, small dice

4 ounces celery, small dice

4 ounces white onion, peeled, small dice

2 tablespoons Paul Prudhomme's Meat Magic

2 tablespoons extra virgin olive oil

1 pound Velveeta cheese

4 ounces sharp cheddar cheese, grated

4 ounces mozzarella cheese, grated

4 ounces Fontinella cheese, grated

4 ounces Asiago cheese, grated

1 teaspoon sea salt

½ teaspoon ground white pepper

Pinch of cayenne pepper

1 teaspoon celery salt

1 teaspoon chili powder

1 cup organic beef stock

PROCEDURE:

1. In a mixing bowl, fold together the hot sausage, green bell pepper, red bell pepper, celery, and onion with the Paul Prudhomme's Meat Magic and olive oil until thoroughly combined.
2. In a nonstick sauté pan over high heat, begin cooking the sausage and vegetable mixture.
3. While the sausage mixture is cooking, add the Velveeta cheese to a Crock-Pot on high setting and allow to melt for about 5 minutes.
4. After 5 minutes, add the grated cheddar cheese, mozzarella cheese, Fontinella cheese, and Asiago cheese to the Crock-Pot.
5. When the sausage is cooked, transfer the sausage and vegetable mixture to the Crock-Pot with the cheeses.
6. Season the dip in the Crock-Pot with the sea salt, ground white pepper, cayenne pepper, celery salt, and chili powder. Stir to combine all ingredients, and allow to cook in Crock-Pot for 45 minutes.
7. After 45 minutes, fold in the beef stock to emulsify the dip. Turn the Crock-Pot down to the low setting and allow an additional 15 minutes of cooking.
8. After 15 minutes, turn the Crock-Pot setting to the *keep warm* setting and serve with assorted crackers.

Artichoke and Spinach Dip

Yield: 10 servings

1 tablespoon extra virgin olive oil

5 ounces baby spinach

13½ ounces quartered artichoke hearts, drained and chopped

2 ounces sun-dried tomatoes, brunoise

3 ounces Fontina cheese, grated

3 ounces mozzarella cheese, grated

2 ounces Asiago cheese, grated

½ cup sour cream

2 cups mayonnaise

1 teaspoon sea salt

Pinch of white pepper

Pinch of celery salt

Pinch of cayenne pepper

¼ cup organic vegetable stock

PROCEDURE:

1. Heat a medium-sized sauté pan over medium-high heat for 10-15 seconds; add the olive oil and sauté the spinach until it wilts.
2. Transfer the wilted spinach to a dinner plate and refrigerate to chill completely.
3. After the spinach is chilled, squeeze as much liquid from it as possible and roughly chop.
4. In a large mixing bowl, fold together the chopped spinach, chopped artichoke hearts, sun-dried tomatoes, Fontina cheese, mozzarella cheese, Asiago cheese, sour cream, mayonnaise, sea salt, white pepper, celery salt, and cayenne pepper until thoroughly combined.
5. Transfer the dip to a microwave-safe bowl and cover with plastic wrap.
6. Microwave on high for 2½ minutes at a time, letting the dip rest out of the microwave for 1 minute after each 2½-minute session. Total microwaving time for dip to heat throughout will be about 7½ minutes.
7. After dip is hot, fold in the vegetable stock to emulsify and serve with pita chips or corn chips.

Goldfish-Crusted Cheesy Potatoes

Yield: 12 servings

1½ pounds thick-sliced bacon

12 ounces white onion, peeled, small dice

10 ounces sour cream

2 cups mayonnaise

½ pint heavy cream

8 ounces colby cheese, small dice

3 large eggs

1 tablespoon sea salt

1 tablespoon fresh cracked black pepper

1 bag (30 ounces) hash brown potatoes, thawed

3 cups Pepperidge Farm cheddar Goldfish snack crackers, crushed

PROCEDURE:

1. Stack the strips of bacon on top of each other and place in freezer for 15 minutes. Remove from freezer and medium dice bacon while it is still partially frozen.
2. In a dry nonstick sauté pan over low heat, slowly render the bacon.
3. When the bacon is beginning to become crispy, add the onions to the pan.
4. Sauté the bacon and onions until the bacon is crispy and fully rendered. Remove from the pan, drain, and discard the excess fat.
5. In a mixing bowl, fold together the sour cream, mayonnaise, heavy cream, colby cheese, eggs, sea salt, and cracked black pepper until thoroughly combined.
6. Add the raw, thawed hash brown potatoes and drained bacon and onions to the sour cream mixture and fold together until all ingredients are thoroughly combined.
7. Evenly spread potato mixture into a sprayed 13"x9" baking pan and evenly coat the top of the potatoes with the crumbled Goldfish snack crackers.
8. Bake the potatoes in a 350-degree oven for 45 minutes.
9. Allow potatoes to rest at room temperature for at least 10 minutes before serving.

Bacon Mushroom Cheeseburger Casserole

Yield: 12 servings

1½ pounds thick-sliced bacon

10 ounces crimini mushrooms, stems removed, quartered

8 ounces white onion, peeled, medium dice

2½ pounds ground beef

1 tablespoon sea salt

1 teaspoon ground white pepper

Dash of cayenne pepper

5 cups heavy cream

18 large eggs

12 ounces sharp cheddar cheese, small dice

1 package sandwich buns (8 buns), large dice

PROCEDURE:

1. Stack the strips of bacon on top of each other and place in freezer for 15 minutes. Remove from freezer and medium dice bacon while it is still partially frozen.
2. In a dry nonstick sauté pan over medium-high heat, render the bacon for 5–7 minutes, until it begins to take on color.
3. When the bacon begins to take on color, add the mushrooms to the pan with the bacon and cook for about 10 minutes, until bacon is almost fully cooked.
4. After 10 minutes, add the onions to the pan and cook an additional 5 minutes, until the onions begin to caramelize.
5. When the onions begin to caramelize, add the ground beef to the pan and season with sea salt, ground white pepper, and cayenne pepper. Stir continuously after adding the beef, and cook for about 4–5 minutes, just until the ground beef is browned.
6. When the ground beef is browned, transfer the contents of the pan to a colander, drain excess fat, and discard.
7. Divide the beef mixture into 2 equal portions, spread flat onto 2 sheet trays, and refrigerate to cool to at least room temperature.
8. While the beef mixture is cooling, prepare the custard by whisking together the heavy cream and eggs in a mixing bowl until thoroughly combined.
9. When the beef mixture is cooled, assemble the casserole in a sprayed 13"x9" baking pan by first spreading an even layer of the beef mixture in the bottom of the pan. Use one full sheet pan of the beef mixture (it was earlier separated into 2 equal portions).

10. Next, evenly layer the diced sharp cheddar cheese on top of the beef mixture.
11. Layer the diced sandwich buns on top of the cheese mixture; lightly press the buns to form an even layer.
12. Layer the second half of the beef mixture onto the layer of diced sandwich buns.
13. Slowly ladle the custard onto the casserole, allowing it to soak in evenly before adding more. Add all of the custard and lightly poke through the casserole with your fingers to allow the custard to soak all the way through.
14. Bake the casserole in a 350-degree oven for 1 hour and 15 minutes, until the custard is fully set up.
15. Allow the casserole to rest at room temperature for at least 15 minutes before cutting and serving.

CHEDDAR-MUSTARD CREAM SAUCE (OPTIONAL FOR CASSEROLE)
Yield: 10–12 servings

1 cup heavy cream
1 tablespoon Dijon mustard
1 teaspoon whole-grain mustard
1 teaspoon honey
2 ounces medium cheddar cheese, small dice
1 tablespoon slurry
Dash of cayenne pepper
Sea salt to taste
Ground white pepper to taste

PROCEDURE:
1. In a saucepan over medium heat, combine the heavy cream, Dijon mustard, whole-grain mustard, and honey and bring to a simmer.
2. When the sauce comes to a simmer, whisk in the cheddar cheese, one piece at a time, until it is all incorporated and melted into the sauce.
3. Add the slurry to thicken slightly; remove from heat; and season with cayenne pepper, sea salt, and ground white pepper to taste.

BACON MUSHROOM CHEESEBURGER CASSEROLE

Italian Pinwheels

Yield: 8 servings

1 tablespoon extra virgin olive oil

1 teaspoon organic butter

8 ounces baby portobello mushrooms, stems removed, sliced

⅔ ounce fresh basil, stems removed, chopped

½ teaspoon garlic, peeled and minced

14 ounces pizza sauce, from a jar

½ cup sour cream

4 ounces Ricotta cheese

2 ounces Asiago cheese, grated

2 ounces Parmesan cheese, grated

½ teaspoon sea salt

Dash of ground white pepper

Dash of cayenne pepper

1 package pizza dough, thin style works the best

2 ounces Provolone cheese, sliced and then each slice cut in half

2 ounces capicola, sliced thin

2 ounces sopressata, sliced thin

2 ounces sandwich pepperoni, sliced thin

2 ounces prosciutto, sliced thin

1½ ounces banana peppers, from a jar

½ teaspoon garlic salt

Dash of fresh cracked black pepper

½ packet of Italian dressing seasoning mix

PROCEDURE:

1. Heat a sauté pan over high heat for 10-15 seconds, add the olive oil and butter, and sauté the mushrooms with the basil and garlic. The mushrooms should be sautéed for about 5 minutes until they are cooked and golden brown.
2. Transfer the mushrooms onto a dinner plate and refrigerate until they are completely chilled.
3. While the mushrooms are cooling, in a mixing bowl whisk together the pizza sauce, sour cream, Ricotta cheese, Asiago cheese, Parmesan cheese, sea salt, ground white pepper, and cayenne pepper.
4. Lay the pizza dough out flat on a cutting board and spread a thin layer of the pizza sauce mixture over the surface of the crust.

5. Layer the Provolone cheese, capicola, sopressata, pepperoni, and prosciutto evenly in layers onto the sauce. The layers should be in the order they are stated, with one on top of the other.
6. Sprinkle the banana peppers and chilled mushrooms onto the meats in an even layer and season the top with the garlic salt and cracked black pepper.
7. Roll the dough from end to end like you would roll a jellyroll or nut roll.
8. Carefully slice the roll into 8 equal-sized pieces and place on a sprayed baking sheet. Be sure to work quickly and use a very sharp knife to slice the roll.

    *To make slicing the roll easier, place the roll into the refrigerator or freezer for 30 – 45 minutes. The colder the roll the easier it is to slice. Be very careful to not freeze the roll while chilling.

9. Bake pinwheels on a sprayed baking sheet in a 350-degree oven for 20 minutes, until the crust is golden brown.
10. Let the baked pinwheels rest at room temperature for at least 10 minutes before serving.
11. For a dipping sauce, use the remainder of the sauce prepared for the pinwheels and whisk in ½ packet of Italian dressing seasoning mix and serve on the side for dipping.

ITALIAN PINWHEELS

THE BAD 179

Asian-Style Chicken Wings

Yield: 2 pounds of chicken wings

FOR THE ASIAN WING SAUCE:

1 cup soy sauce

¼ cup honey

1 teaspoon Sriracha chili sauce

Pinch of red pepper flakes

2 tablespoons slurry

PROCEDURE:

1. In a saucepan over medium-high heat, whisk together the soy sauce, honey, Sriracha, and red pepper flakes and bring to a boil.
2. When the sauce comes to a boil, add the slurry to thicken and remove from heat. Cool the sauce to room temperature before using on wings.

FOR THE ASIAN-STYLE CHICKEN WINGS:

1 tablespoon chili powder

1 teaspoon celery salt

Pinch of ground white pepper

⅓ cup all-purpose flour

2 pounds chicken wings

1 recipe Asian wing sauce (see earlier recipe)

PROCEDURE:

1. In a mixing bowl, combine the chili powder, celery salt, ground white pepper, and flour and mix to thoroughly combine.
2. Add the chicken wings to the dry rub and mix thoroughly until completely coated.
3. Deep-fry the wings in either canola or peanut oil at 350 degrees for 15 minutes. They should be golden brown and have an internal temperature of at least 165 degrees.
4. In a large mixing bowl, toss the wings with the Asian wing sauce and serve.

About the Authors

MARIO J. PORRECA

Mario J. Porreca attended Westmoreland County Community College, where he majored in Culinary Arts, and completed a three-year apprenticeship at the Duquesne Club in Pittsburgh, Pennsylvania. The Duquesne Club is a very prestigious city club and has been given the designation of the No. 1 City Club in America in 1997, 2001, 2003, and 2006. Mario completed his apprenticeship there and stayed on full-time for another 2½ years. He was promoted to sous chef, where he managed under executive chef Keith Coughenour for 1½ years. He then discovered nutritional cleansing, and it changed his life forever. Through nutritional cleansing, Mario released 70 pounds in 5½ months and realized that sharing this technology with the world was also a passion of his. Mario now teaches people how to cleanse to better their health and is also the founder of Mario's Menu. Through Mario's Menu, Mario and his associates educate people on the importance of health and nutrition through proper diet and nutritional cleansing. Mario can be reached directly at mario@mariosmenu.com.

KIRK KOLICH

Kirk Kolich is a corporate executive chef for Parkhurst Dining Services. Kirk began his career in the culinary field in 1992 at Dante's Restaurant in Herminie, Pennsylvania. He then cooked at the Laurel Valley Golf Club in Ligonier, Pennsylvania, before graduating from the Culinary Institute of America in Hyde Park, New York, in 1995. He did his externship at The Breakers in Palm Beach, Florida. While working at The Breakers, Kirk worked all stations in the 5-Star, 5-Diamond hotel resort. Upon completion of his externship, he then went on to work at the Duquesne Club in Pittsburgh, Pennsylvania, where he was soon promoted to executive sous chef. While at the Duquesne Club, Kirk managed a staff of 40 chefs and cooks; catered private parties; and created menus for private catering events, wine tastings, the health and fitness center, and two separate fine-dining rooms. Kirk also attended a class on Nouvelle Cuisine with the late Jean-Louis Palladin at the Culinary Institute of America in Napa Valley, California, in July 2003. Kirk resides in North Huntingdon, Pennsylvania, and can be reached directly via email at kirk@mariosmenu.com.

JOSEPH D. PORRECA, BS, DC

Dr. Joseph D. Porreca has been practicing chiropractic medicine in Belle Vernon, Pennsylvania, since 1985. Dr. Porreca graduated from California University of Pennsylvania with a bachelor's degree in Biology before he went on to graduate summa cum laude from Palmer College of Chiropractic in Davenport, Iowa. In addition to practicing chiropractic medicine, Dr. Porreca is also board eligible in Neurology. Dr. Porreca discovered the technology of nutritional cleansing over two years ago and experienced amazing results himself before implementing it into his chiropractic practice.

Dr. Porreca has been married to his wife Denise for the past 29 years and has one son and one daughter. Dr. Porreca is the owner/clinic director of Porreca Chiropractic Center in Belle Vernon, Pennsylvania. He can be reached directly by email at drjoe@mariosmenu.com.

For additional information or questions that you may have, Mario's Menu, LLC can be reached via their website at www.mariosmenu.com, by email at info@mariosmenu.com, or by phone at (800) 531-7531.

All recipe content and photography ©Mario's Menu, LLC all rights reserved.